MATTHEW

The Coming of the King

JOHN MACARTHUR

THOMAS NELSON
Since 1798

MATTHEW
MACARTHUR BIBLE STUDIES

© 2007, John MacArthur.

All rights reserved. No portion of this book may be reproduced, stored in a retrieval system, or transmitted in any form or by any means—electronic, mechanical, photocopy, recording, or any other—except for brief quotations in printed reviews, without the prior permission of the publisher.

John MacArthur
"Unleashing God's Truth, One Verse at at a Time®"
"Unleashing God's Truth, One Verse at a Time" is a trademark of Grace to You. All rights reserved.

Published in Nashville, Tennessee, by Nelson Books, an imprint of Thomas Nelson. Nelson Books and Thomas Nelson are registered trademarks of HarperCollins Christian Publishing, Inc.

Nelson Books titles may be purchased in bulk for education, business, fundraising, or sales promotional use. For information, please email SpecialMarkets@ThomasNelson.com

Produced with the assistance of the Livingstone Corporation. Project staff include Jake Barton, Mary Horner Collins, and Andy Culbertson.

Project editor: Len Woods

Scripture quotations marked NKJV are taken from *The Holy Bible*, New King James Version®. © 1979, 1980, 1982, 1992 Thomas Nelson, Inc. Publishers.

"Keys to the Text" material taken from the following sources:

The MacArthur Study Bible (electronic ed.), John MacArthur, General Editor. © 1997 by Word Publishing. All rights reserved. Used by permission.

Matthew, 1–7, 8–15, 16–23, 24–28 (electronic ed.). MacArthur New Testament Commentary Series. © 1989 by John MacArthur. Published by Moody Press, Chicago, Illinois. Used by permission.

Nelson's New Illustrated Bible Dictionary, Rev. ed. R. F. Youngblood, F. F. Bruce, R. K. Harrison, editors. © 1995 by Thomas Nelson Publishers.

Cover Art by Holly Sharp Design
Interior Design and Composition by Joel Bartlett, Livingstone Corporation

ISBN 978-0-7180-3501-3

Printed in the United States of America.
HB 05.01.2024

CONTENTS

INTRODUCTION TO MATTHEW

Matthew, meaning "gift of the Lord," was the other name of Levi (9:9), the tax collector who left everything to follow Christ (Luke 5:27, 28). Matthew was one of the twelve apostles (10:3; Mark 3:18; Luke 6:15; Acts 1:13). In his own list of the twelve disciples, he explicitly calls himself a "tax collector" (10:3). Nowhere else in Scripture is the name Matthew associated with "tax collector"; the other evangelists always employ his former name, Levi, when speaking of his sinful past. This is evidence of humility on Matthew's part. As with the other three Gospels, this work is known by the name of its author.

AUTHOR AND DATE

The canonicity and Matthean authorship of this gospel were unchallenged in the early church. Eusebius (ca. AD 265–339) quotes Origen (ca. AD 185–254): "Among the four Gospels, which are the only indisputable ones in the church of God under heaven, I have learned by tradition that the first was written by Matthew, who was once a publican, but afterwards an apostle of Jesus Christ, and it was prepared for the converts from Judaism" (*Ecclesiastical History*, 6:25). It is clear that this Gospel was written at a relatively early date—prior to the destruction of the temple in AD 70. Some scholars have proposed a date as early as AD 50.

BACKGROUND AND SETTING

The Jewish flavor of Matthew's gospel is remarkable. This is evident even in the opening genealogy, which Matthew traces back only as far as Abraham. In contrast, Luke, aiming to show Christ as the Redeemer of humanity, goes all the way back to Adam. Matthew's purpose is somewhat narrower: to demonstrate that Christ is the King and Messiah of Israel. This Gospel quotes more than sixty times from Old Testament prophetic passages, emphasizing how Christ is the fulfillment of all those promises.

The probability that Matthew's audience was predominantly Jewish is further evident from several facts. Matthew usually cites Jewish custom without explaining it, in contrast to the other Gospels (see Mark 7:3; John 19:40). He constantly refers to Christ as "the Son of David" (1:1; 9:27; 12:23; 15:22; 20:30; 21:9, 15; 22:42, 45). Matthew even guards Jewish sensibilities regarding the name

1

of God, referring to "the kingdom of heaven" where the other evangelists speak of "the kingdom of God." All the book's major themes are rooted in the Old Testament and set in light of Israel's messianic expectations.

Matthew's use of Greek may suggest that he was writing as a Palestinian Jew to Hellenistic Jews elsewhere. He wrote as an eyewitness of many of the events he described, giving firsthand testimony about the words and works of Jesus of Nazareth.

His purpose is clear: to demonstrate that Jesus is the Jewish nation's long-awaited Messiah. His voluminous quoting of the Old Testament is specifically designed to show the tie between the Messiah of promise and the Christ of history. This purpose is never out of focus for Matthew, and he even adduces many incidental details from the Old Testament prophecies as proof of Jesus' messianic claims (e.g., 2:17, 18; 4:13–15; 13:35; 21:4–5; 27:9–10).

HISTORICAL AND THEOLOGICAL THEMES

Since Matthew is concerned with setting forth Jesus as Messiah, the King of the Jews, a recurring theme throughout this Gospel is an interest in the Old Testament kingdom promises. Matthew's signature phrase, "the kingdom of heaven," occurs thirty-two times in this book (and nowhere else in all of Scripture).

The opening genealogy is designed to document Christ's credentials as Israel's king, and the rest of the book completes this theme. Matthew shows that Christ is the heir of the kingly line. He demonstrates that He is the fulfillment of dozens of Old Testament prophecies regarding the king who would come. He offers evidence after evidence to establish Christ's kingly prerogative. All other historical and theological themes in the book revolve around this one.

Matthew records five major discourses: the Sermon on the Mount (chs. 5–7); the commissioning of the apostles (ch. 10); the parables about the kingdom (ch. 13); a discourse about the childlikeness of the believer (ch. 18); and the discourse on His second coming (chs. 24, 25). Each discourse ends with a variation of this phrase: "when Jesus had ended these sayings" (7:28; 11:1; 13:53; 19:1; 26:1). That becomes a motif signaling a new narrative portion. A long opening section (chs. 1–4) and a short conclusion (28:16–20) bracket the rest of the Gospel, which naturally divides into five sections, each with a discourse and a narrative section. Some have seen a parallel between these five sections and the five books of Moses in the Old Testament.

The conflict between Christ and Pharisaism is another common theme in Matthew's Gospel. But Matthew is keen to show the error of the Pharisees for the benefit of his Jewish audience—but not for personal or self-aggrandizing reasons. Matthew omits, for example, the parable of the Pharisee and the tax collector, even though that parable would have put him in a favorable light.

Matthew also mentions the Sadducees more than any of the other Gospels. Both Pharisees and Sadducees are regularly portrayed negatively, and held up as warning beacons. Their doctrine is a leaven that must be avoided (16:11–12). Although these groups were doctrinally at odds with each other, they were united in their hatred of Christ. To Matthew, they epitomized all in Israel who rejected Christ as King.

The rejection of Israel's Messiah is another constant theme in this Gospel. In no other Gospel are the attacks against Jesus portrayed as strongly as here. From the flight into Egypt to the scene at the cross, Matthew paints a more vivid portrayal of Christ's rejection than any of the other evangelists. In Matthew's account of the crucifixion, for example, no thief repents, and no friends or loved ones are seen at the foot of the cross. In His death, He is forsaken even by God (27:46). The shadow of rejection is never lifted from the story.

Yet Matthew portrays Him as a victorious King who will one day return "on the clouds of heaven with power and great glory" (24:30).

INTERPRETIVE CHALLENGES

As noted above, Matthew groups his narrative material around five great discourses. He makes no attempt to follow a strict chronology, and a comparison of the Gospels reveals that Matthew freely places things out of order. He is dealing with themes and broad concepts, not laying out a timeline.

The prophetic passages present a particular interpretive challenge. Jesus' Olivet discourse, for example, contains some details that evoke images of the violent destruction of Jerusalem in AD 70. Jesus' words in 24:34 have led some to conclude that all these things were fulfilled—albeit not literally—in the Roman conquest of that era. This is the view known as "preterism." But this is a serious interpretive blunder, forcing the interpreter to read into these passages spiritualized, allegorical meanings unwarranted by normal exegetical methods. The grammatical-historical hermeneutical approach to these passages is the approach to follow, and it yields a consistently futuristic interpretation of crucial prophecies.

NOTES

_____

THE COMING OF THE KING

Matthew 1:1–2:23

DRAWING NEAR

The Gospel of Matthew opens with the miracle of Jesus' birth! Describe some of the Christmas activities and traditions you and your family observe.

_____

_____

_____

If someone from another culture (unfamiliar with the significance of the holiday) visited you during this time, what would he or she conclude about the meaning of Christmas?

_____

_____

_____

THE CONTEXT

Matthew records the good news about the most significant events in all of history—the birth, life, sacrificial death, and resurrection of Jesus of Nazareth. Each Gospel writer wrote from a unique perspective and for a different audience. As a result, each Gospel contains distinctive elements. Taken together, the four Gospels form a complete testimony about Jesus Christ.

Matthew wrote primarily to a Jewish audience, presenting Jesus of Nazareth as Israel's long-awaited Messiah and rightful King. He opens his book with a genealogy which, unlike Luke's, focuses on Jesus' royal descent from Israel's greatest king, David. The primary purpose of chapters one and two is to establish Jesus' right to Israel's kingship. To any honest observer, and certainly to Jews who knew and believed their own Scriptures, these two chapters vindicate Jesus' claim before Pilate: "You say rightly that I am a king. For this cause I was born, and for this cause I have come into the world" (John 18:37 NKJV).

Consistent with this purpose of revealing Jesus to be the Christ (Messiah) and the King of the Jews, Matthew begins his Gospel by showing Jesus' lineage from the royal line of Israel. If Jesus is to be heralded and proclaimed King, there must be proof that He comes from the recognized royal family.

KEYS TO THE TEXT

Gospel: The English word *gospel* derives from the Anglo-Saxon word *godspell*, which can mean either "a story about God" or "a good story." The latter meaning is in harmony with the Greek word *euangellion,* which means "good news." Matthew and the other Gospels record the good news of Jesus' life. They are not biographies in the modern sense of the word, since they do not intend to present a complete life of Jesus. Apart from the birth narratives, they give little information about the first thirty years of Jesus' life. Though they are completely accurate historically and present important biographical details of Jesus' life, the primary purposes of the Gospels are theological and apologetic. They provide authoritative answers to questions about Jesus' life and ministry, and they strengthen believers' assurance regarding the reality of their faith.

Kingdom of Heaven: This refers to the place where God rules and reigns. Matthew alone uses this phrase, avoiding the parallel phrase "kingdom of God" because of the unbiblical connotations it had in first-century Jewish thought. Matthew wrote his Gospel, then, to strengthen the faith of Jewish Christians, and it provides a useful apologetic tool for Jewish evangelism.

UNLEASHING THE TEXT

Read 1:1–2:23, noting the key words and definitions next to the passage.

Son of David (v. 1)—a messianic title used as such in only Matthew, Mark, and Luke

Tamar (v. 4)—It is unusual for women to be named in genealogies. Tamar, Rahab, and Ruth (v. 5), Bathsheba ("Uriah's wife," v. 6), and Mary (v. 16) are each an object lesson about the workings of divine grace.

Salmon begot Boaz by Rahab . . . and Jesse begot David the king (vv. 5–6)—Matthew's genealogy sometimes skips over several generations between well-known characters in order to abbreviate the listing.

Matthew 1:1–2:23 (NKJV)

1 *The book of the genealogy of Jesus Christ, the Son of David, the Son of Abraham:*

2 *Abraham begot Isaac, Isaac begot Jacob, and Jacob begot Judah and his brothers.*

3 *Judah begot Perez and Zerah by Tamar, Perez begot Hezron, and Hezron begot Ram.*

4 *Ram begot Amminadab, Amminadab begot Nahshon, and Nahshon begot Salmon.*

5 *Salmon begot Boaz by Rahab, Boaz begot Obed by Ruth, Obed begot Jesse,*

6 *and Jesse begot David the king. David the king begot Solomon by her who had been the wife of Uriah.*

7 *Solomon begot Rehoboam, Rehoboam begot Abijah, and Abijah begot Asa.*

8 *Asa begot Jehoshaphat, Jehoshaphat begot Joram, and Joram begot Uzziah.*

9 Uzziah begot Jotham, Jotham begot Ahaz, and Ahaz begot Hezekiah.

10 Hezekiah begot Manasseh, Manasseh begot Amon, and Amon begot Josiah.

11 Josiah begot Jeconiah and his brothers about the time they were carried away to Babylon.

12 And after they were brought to Babylon, Jeconiah begot Shealtiel, and Shealtiel begot Zerubbabel.

13 Zerubbabel begot Abiud, Abiud begot Eliakim, and Eliakim begot Azor.

14 Azor begot Zadok, Zadok begot Achim, and Achim begot Eliud.

15 Eliud begot Eleazar, Eleazar begot Matthan, and Matthan begot Jacob.

16 And Jacob begot Joseph the husband of Mary, of whom was born Jesus who is called Christ.

17 So all the generations from Abraham to David are fourteen generations, from David until the captivity in Babylon are fourteen generations, and from the captivity in Babylon until the Christ are fourteen generations.

18 Now the birth of Jesus Christ was as follows: After His mother Mary was betrothed to Joseph, before they came together, she was found with child of the Holy Spirit.

19 Then Joseph her husband, being a just man, and not wanting to make her a public example, was minded to put her away secretly.

20 But while he thought about these things, behold, an angel of the Lord appeared to him in a dream, saying, "Joseph, son of David, do not be afraid to take to you Mary your wife, for that which is conceived in her is of the Holy Spirit.

21 And she will bring forth a Son, and you shall call His name JESUS, for He will save His people from their sins."

22 So all this was done that it might be fulfilled which was spoken by the Lord through the prophet, saying:

23 "Behold, the virgin shall be with child, and bear a Son, and they shall call His name Immanuel," which is translated, "God with us."

Joseph the husband of Mary, of whom was born Jesus (v. 16)—The only entry in the entire genealogy where the word *begot* is not used—underscoring the fact that Jesus was not Joseph's literal offspring, but nonetheless establishing His claim to the throne of David as Joseph's legal heir.

betrothed (v. 18)—Jewish betrothal was as binding as modern marriage. A divorce was necessary to terminate the betrothal (v. 19), and the betrothed couple were regarded legally as husband and wife (v. 19), although physical union had not yet taken place.

Joseph . . . being a just *man* . . . was minded to put her away secretly (v. 19)—Stoning was the legal prescription for adultery (see Deut. 22:23–24). The phrase "a just man" is a Hebraism suggesting that Joseph was a true believer in God who carefully obeyed the law (see Gen. 6:9). To "put her [Mary] away" would be to obtain a legal divorce (19:8–9; Deut. 24:1).

an angel of the Lord (v. 20)—one of only a few such angelic visitations in the New Testament, most of which are associated with Christ's birth

JESUS (v. 21)—The name actually means "Savior."

virgin (v. 23)—While scholars dispute whether the Hebrew term in Isaiah 7:14 means "virgin" or "maiden," Matthew quotes here from the LXX, which uses the unambiguous Greek term for "virgin."

know her (v. 25)—a euphemism for sexual intercourse. See Gen. 4:1, 17, 25; 38:26; Judges 11:39.

Bethlehem (2:1)—a small village on the southern outskirts of Jerusalem, which Hebrew scholars in Jesus' day clearly expected to be the birthplace of the Messiah (see Mic. 5:2; John 7:42).

wise men from the East (v. 1) —not kings, but Magi, magicians, or astrologers—possibly Zoroastrian scholars from Persia whose knowledge of the Hebrew Scriptures could be traced back to the time of Daniel (Dan. 5:11). Their number is not given—the traditional notion that there were three stems from the number of gifts they brought.

star (v. 2)—not a supernova or a conjunction of planets, as some modern theories suggest, because of the way the star moved and settled over one place (see v. 9); more likely a supernatural reality similar to the Shekinah that guided the Israelites in the days of Moses (Ex. 13:21)

scribes (v. 4)—primarily Pharisees, i.e., authorities on Jewish law. Sometimes they are referred to as "lawyers."

that I may come and worship Him (v. 8)—Herod actually wanted to kill the child (vv. 13–18), whom he saw as a potential threat to his throne.

into the house (v. 11)—By the time the wise men arrived, Mary and Joseph were situated in a house, not a stable (see Luke 2:7).

24 Then Joseph, being aroused from sleep, did as the angel of the Lord commanded him and took to him his wife,

25 and did not know her till she had brought forth her firstborn Son. And he called His name JESUS.

2:1 Now after Jesus was born in Bethlehem of Judea in the days of Herod the king, behold, wise men from the East came to Jerusalem,

2 saying, "Where is He who has been born King of the Jews? For we have seen His star in the East and have come to worship Him."

3 When Herod the king heard this, he was troubled, and all Jerusalem with him.

4 And when he had gathered all the chief priests and scribes of the people together, he inquired of them where the Christ was to be born.

5 So they said to him, "In Bethlehem of Judea, for thus it is written by the prophet:

6 'But you, Bethlehem, in the land of Judah, Are not the least among the rulers of Judah; For out of you shall come a Ruler Who will shepherd My people Israel.' "

7 Then Herod, when he had secretly called the wise men, determined from them what time the star appeared.

8 And he sent them to Bethlehem and said, "Go and search carefully for the young Child, and when you have found Him, bring back word to me, that I may come and worship Him also."

9 When they heard the king, they departed; and behold, the star which they had seen in the East went before them, till it came and stood over where the young Child was.

10 When they saw the star, they rejoiced with exceedingly great joy.

11 And when they had come into the house, they saw the young Child with Mary His mother, and fell down and worshiped Him. And when they had opened their treasures, they presented gifts to Him: gold, frankincense, and myrrh.

12 *Then, being divinely warned in a dream that they should not return to Herod, they departed for their own country another way.*

13 *Now when they had departed, behold, an angel of the Lord appeared to Joseph in a dream, saying, "Arise, take the young Child and His mother, flee to Egypt, and stay there until I bring you word; for Herod will seek the young Child to destroy Him."*

14 *When he arose, he took the young Child and His mother by night and departed for Egypt,*

15 *and was there until the death of Herod, that it might be fulfilled which was spoken by the Lord through the prophet, saying, "Out of Egypt I called My Son."*

16 *Then Herod, when he saw that he was deceived by the wise men, was exceedingly angry; and he sent forth and put to death all the male children who were in Bethlehem and in all its districts, from two years old and under, according to the time which he had determined from the wise men.*

17 *Then was fulfilled what was spoken by Jeremiah the prophet, saying:*

18 *"A voice was heard in Ramah, Lamentation, weeping, and great mourning, Rachel weeping for her children, Refusing to be comforted, Because they are no more."*

19 *Now when Herod was dead, behold, an angel of the Lord appeared in a dream to Joseph in Egypt,*

20 *saying, "Arise, take the young Child and His mother, and go to the land of Israel, for those who sought the young Child's life are dead."*

21 *Then he arose, took the young Child and His mother, and came into the land of Israel.*

22 *But when he heard that Archelaus was reigning over Judea instead of his father Herod, he was afraid to go there. And being warned by God in a dream, he turned aside into the region of Galilee.*

23 *And he came and dwelt in a city called Nazareth, that it might be fulfilled which was spoken by the prophets, "He shall be called a Nazarene."*

the death of Herod (v. 15)—Recent scholarship sets this date at 4 BC. It is probable that the stay in Egypt was very brief—perhaps no more than a few weeks.

Out of Egypt (v. 15)—This quotation is from Hosea 11:1, which speaks of God's leading Israel out of Egypt in the Exodus. Matthew suggests that Israel's sojourn in Egypt was a pictorial prophecy, rather than a specific verbal one such as v. 6 (see 1:23). These are called "types," and all are always fulfilled in Christ and identified clearly by the New Testament writers. Another example of a type is found in John 3:14.

Archelaus (v. 22)—Herod's kingdom was divided among his three sons: Archelaus ruled Judea, Samaria, and Idumea; Herod Philip II ruled the regions north of Galilee (Luke 3:1); and Herod Antipas ruled Galilee and Perea (Luke 3:1). History records that Archelaus was so brutal and ineffective that he was deposed by Rome after a short reign and replaced with a governor appointed by Rome. Pontius Pilate was the fifth governor of Judea. Herod Antipas is the main Herod in the gospel accounts. He had John the Baptist put to death (14:1–12) and examined Christ on the eve of the crucifixion (Luke 23:7–12).

"He shall be called a Nazarene" (v. 23)—Nazareth was an obscure town 55 miles north of Jerusalem, a place of lowly reputation, and nowhere mentioned in the Old Testament. "Nazarene" was a synonym for someone who is despised or detestable—that was how people from the region were often characterized (see John 1:46).

1) Looking back over chapter 1, what are some of the titles and descriptions used to describe Jesus?

_____

_____

_____

_____

_____

2) What do these chapters reveal about Joseph, the "stepfather" of Christ?

_____

_____

_____

_____

_____

_____

3) How did Herod respond to the news of Jesus' birth?

_____

_____

_____

_____

_____

4) How do our traditions about "the wise men" compare with what the biblical text actually says?

_____

_____

_____

_____

GOING DEEPER

Read Luke 2:1–20, the other account of the coming of Christ into the world.

1 *And it came to pass in those days that a decree went out from Caesar Augustus that all the world should be registered.*

2 *This census first took place while Quirinius was governing Syria.*

3 *So all went to be registered, everyone to his own city.*

4 *Joseph also went up from Galilee, out of the city of Nazareth, into Judea, to the city of David, which is called Bethlehem, because he was of the house and lineage of David,*

5 *to be registered with Mary, his betrothed wife, who was with child.*

6 *So it was, that while they were there, the days were completed for her to be delivered.*

7 *And she brought forth her firstborn Son, and wrapped Him in swaddling cloths, and laid Him in a manger, because there was no room for them in the inn.*

8 *Now there were in the same country shepherds living out in the fields, keeping watch over their flock by night.*

9 *And behold, an angel of the Lord stood before them, and the glory of the Lord shone around them, and they were greatly afraid.*

10 *Then the angel said to them, "Do not be afraid, for behold, I bring you good tidings of great joy which will be to all people.*

11 *For there is born to you this day in the city of David a Savior, who is Christ the Lord.*

12 *And this will be the sign to you: You will find a Babe wrapped in swaddling cloths, lying in a manger."*

13 *And suddenly there was with the angel a multitude of the heavenly host praising God and saying:*

14 *"Glory to God in the highest, And on earth peace, goodwill toward men!"*

15 *So it was, when the angels had gone away from them into heaven, that the shepherds said to one another, "Let us now go to Bethlehem and see this thing that has come to pass, which the Lord has made known to us."*

16 *And they came with haste and found Mary and Joseph, and the Babe lying in a manger.*

17 *Now when they had seen Him, they made widely known the saying which was told them concerning this Child.*

18 *And all those who heard it marveled at those things which were told them by the shepherds.*

19 *But Mary kept all these things and pondered them in her heart.*

20 *Then the shepherds returned, glorifying and praising God for all the things that they had heard and seen, as it was told them.*

Exploring the Meaning

5) What new details or insights do you find in Luke 2, to add to your growing understanding of the Incarnation—God becoming flesh in the person of Christ?

_____

_____

_____

_____

6) Why does Matthew begin his Gospel with the genealogical records of Christ?

_____

_____

_____

_____

7) What is the significance of the statement that Mary was "found with child of the Holy Spirit" (1:18)?

_____

_____

_____

_____

8) The wise men sought and worshiped Christ; Herod attempted to kill Him. In what ways (if any) are these men representative of people's response to Jesus?

_____

_____

_____

_____

Truth for Today

The supernatural birth of Jesus is the only way to account for the life that He lived. A skeptic who denied the virgin birth once asked a Christian, "If I told you that child over there was born without a human father, would you believe me?" The believer replied, "Yes, if he lived as Jesus lived." The greatest outward evidence of Jesus' supernatural birth and deity is His life.

Reflecting on the Text

9) Mary and Joseph faced a very unusual "crisis." Though she was a virgin, she was pregnant. How do you think others viewed their relationship and treated them? What can modern Christians learn from their response to an extremely trying situation?

_____

_____

_____

_____

10) What are the life lessons we can glean from the "wise men"? See if you can list at least five.

_____

_____

_____

_____

11) In the first two chapters of Matthew you have met some fascinating people—some who honored Christ and served Him, and some who opposed Him fiercely. What two things will you do differently, as a result of this study, to demonstrate your love and devotion to Christ?

_____

_____

_____

_____

12) Compose a short prayer of praise to God, thanking Him for sending Christ the Savior into a dark, dying world.

_____

_____

_____

_____

PERSONAL RESPONSE

Write out additional reflections, questions you may have, or a prayer.

_____

_____

_____

_____

_____

_____

_____

_____

_____

_____

_____

_____

_____

_____

_____

_____

_____

_____

2

THE KING BEGINS TO MINISTER
Matthew 3:1–4:25

DRAWING NEAR

Imagine being there in first-century Palestine when Jesus first came on the scene. If you had to choose three words to describe or characterize Jesus' ministry, what would they be?

_____

_____

_____

THE CONTEXT

In chapter 1, Matthew shows Jesus' kingship by His birth—by His descent from the royal line of David and by His miraculous conception. In chapter 2, Christ's kingship is shown by the circumstances surrounding His birth—by the homage of the magi, the murderous hatred of Herod, and God's miraculous protection of the young Jesus. In chapter 3, Matthew shows more evidence through a God-appointed forerunner named John, who heralded the King's arrival. Following a description of the King's divine commissioning, or coronation (Christ's baptism and anointing by the Spirit), Matthew records the great test of Christ's kingliness in chapter 4. Jesus' rejections of Satan's temptations further demonstrate His divine kingship and His absolute power over hell and sin.

Tested, tried, and triumphant over the evil one, King Jesus inaugurates His public ministry. He begins to preach the good news of the kingdom, to call men to follow Him, and to heal the sick.

KEYS TO THE TEXT

A Herald: In ancient times it was common for a herald to precede the arrival of the monarch, to announce his coming, and to prepare for his safe and proper travel. With a coterie of servants, the herald would make sure that the roadway was as smooth and uncluttered as possible. Holes would be filled, rocks and debris would be removed, and unsightly litter would be burned or hidden. As the group traveled along and worked, the herald would proclaim the king's coming to everyone he encountered. His twofold duty was to proclaim and to prepare. That is what John the Baptist's ministry did for God's great King, Jesus Christ.

Unleashing the Text

Read 3:1–4:25, noting the key words and definitions next to the passage.

Matthew 3:1–4:25 (NKJV)

the wilderness of Judea (3:1)—the region to the immediate west of the Dead Sea—an utterly barren desert, and a seemingly odd location to announce the arrival of a King, but perfectly in keeping with God's mysterious ways

Repent (v. 2)—no mere academic change of mind, nor mere regret or remorse, but a radical turning from sin that inevitably became manifest in the fruit of righteousness (v. 8)

the kingdom of heaven (v. 2)—An expression unique to Matthew's Gospel, this refers to the sphere of God's dominion over those who belong to Him.

clothed in camel's hair, with a leather belt (v. 4)—Practical and long-wearing, but far from comfortable or fashionable, these clothes (and John's behavior) evoke the image of Elijah (2 Kings 1:8).

baptized (v. 6)—John's baptism likely had its roots in Old Testament purification rituals (see Lev. 15:13) and dramatically symbolized repentance in anticipation of the Messiah's arrival.

the wrath to come (v. 7)—John's preaching echoed the familiar Old Testament theme of promised wrath in the Day of the Lord (e.g., Ezek. 7:19; Zeph. 1:18).

fruits worthy of repentance (v. 8)—Repentance and faith are inextricably linked in Scripture, works being the inevitable fruit of conversion.

1 In those days John the Baptist came preaching in the wilderness of Judea,

2 and saying, "Repent, for the kingdom of heaven is at hand!"

3 For this is he who was spoken of by the prophet Isaiah, saying: "The voice of one crying in the wilderness: 'Prepare the way of the LORD; Make His paths straight.' "

4 Now John himself was clothed in camel's hair, with a leather belt around his waist; and his food was locusts and wild honey.

5 Then Jerusalem, all Judea, and all the region around the Jordan went out to him

6 and were baptized by him in the Jordan, confessing their sins.

7 But when he saw many of the Pharisees and Sadducees coming to his baptism, he said to them, "Brood of vipers! Who warned you to flee from the wrath to come?

8 Therefore bear fruits worthy of repentance,

9 and do not think to say to yourselves, 'We have Abraham as our father.' For I say to you that God is able to raise up children to Abraham from these stones.

10 And even now the ax is laid to the root of the trees. Therefore every tree which does not bear good fruit is cut down and thrown into the fire.

11 I indeed baptize you with water unto repentance, but He who is coming after me is mightier than I, whose sandals I am not worthy to carry. He will baptize you with the Holy Spirit and fire.

Abraham as *our* father (v. 9)—The Jews believed that merely being descendants of Abraham, members of God's chosen race, made them spiritually secure.

12 *His winnowing fan is in His hand, and He will thoroughly clean out His threshing floor, and gather His wheat into the barn; but He will burn up the chaff with unquenchable fire."*

13 *Then Jesus came from Galilee to John at the Jordan to be baptized by him.*

14 *And John tried to prevent Him, saying, "I need to be baptized by You, and are You coming to me?"*

15 *But Jesus answered and said to him, "Permit it to be so now, for thus it is fitting for us to fulfill all righteousness." Then he allowed Him.*

16 *When He had been baptized, Jesus came up immediately from the water; and behold, the heavens were opened to Him, and He saw the Spirit of God descending like a dove and alighting upon Him.*

17 *And suddenly a voice came from heaven, saying, "This is My beloved Son, in whom I am well pleased."*

4:1 *Then Jesus was led up by the Spirit into the wilderness to be tempted by the devil*

2 *And when He had fasted forty days and forty nights, afterward He was hungry.*

3 *Now when the tempter came to Him, he said, "If You are the Son of God, command that these stones become bread."*

4 *But He answered and said, "It is written, 'Man shall not live by bread alone, but by every word that proceeds from the mouth of God.'"*

5 *Then the devil took Him up into the holy city, set Him on the pinnacle of the temple,*

6 *and said to Him, "If You are the Son of God, throw Yourself down. For it is written: 'He shall give His angels charge over you,' and, 'In their hands they shall bear you up, Lest you dash your foot against a stone.'"*

7 *Jesus said to him, "It is written again, 'You shall not tempt the LORD your God.'"*

8 *Again, the devil took Him up on an exceedingly high mountain, and showed Him all the kingdoms of the world and their glory.*

winnowing fan (v. 12)—a tool for tossing grain into the wind so that the chaff is blown away

it is fitting for us to fulfill all righteousness (v. 15)—Christ was here identifying Himself with sinners and picturing His eventual death and resurrection (see Luke 12:50).

Jesus . . . the Spirit of God . . . a voice *came from* heaven (vv. 16–17)—All three Persons of the Trinity are clearly delineated.

led up by the Spirit . . . to be tempted by the devil (4:1)—God Himself is never the agent of temptation (James 1:13), but here—as in the book of Job—God uses even satanic tempting to serve His sovereign purposes.

If You are the Son of God (v. 3)—"If" is conditional, meaning "since" in this context. There was no doubt in Satan's mind who Jesus was, but his design was to get Christ to violate God's plan and employ the divine power that He had temporarily set aside when He took on human flesh (see Phil. 2:7).

It is written (v. 4)—All three of Jesus' replies to the devil were taken from Deuteronomy.

For it is written . . . *"Lest you dash your foot against a stone"* (v. 6)—Note how Satan quotes (and twists) Scripture (Ps. 91:11-12), employing a passage about *trusting* God to justify *testing* Him.

I will give You (v. 9)—Satan is both the "ruler of this world" (John 12:31; 14:30; 16:11), and the "god of this age" (2 Cor. 4:4).

John had been put in prison (v. 12)—For his bold rebuke of Herod Antipas, see 14:3–4.

From that time Jesus began to preach (v. 17)—the beginning of His public ministry, His message echoing what John the Baptist had preached

two brothers (v. 18)—Jesus had encountered Peter and Andrew before, near Bethabara, in the Jordan region, where Andrew (and perhaps Peter as well) had become a disciple of John the Baptist (John 1:35–42).

9 And he said to Him, "All these things I will give You if You will fall down and worship me."

10 Then Jesus said to him, "Away with you, Satan! For it is written, 'You shall worship the LORD your God, and Him only you shall serve.' "

11 Then the devil left Him, and behold, angels came and ministered to Him.

12 Now when Jesus heard that John had been put in prison, He departed to Galilee.

13 And leaving Nazareth, He came and dwelt in Capernaum, which is by the sea, in the regions of Zebulun and Naphtali,

14 that it might be fulfilled which was spoken by Isaiah the prophet, saying:

15 "The land of Zebulun and the land of Naphtali, By the way of the sea, beyond the Jordan, Galilee of the Gentiles:

16 The people who sat in darkness have seen a great light, And upon those who sat in the region and shadow of death Light has dawned."

17 From that time Jesus began to preach and to say, "Repent, for the kingdom of heaven is at hand."

18 And Jesus, walking by the Sea of Galilee, saw two brothers, Simon called Peter, and Andrew his brother, casting a net into the sea; for they were fishermen.

19 Then He said to them, "Follow Me, and I will make you fishers of men."

20 They immediately left their nets and followed Him.

21 Going on from there, He saw two other brothers, James the son of Zebedee, and John his brother, in the boat with Zebedee their father, mending their nets. He called them,

22 and immediately they left the boat and their father, and followed Him.

23 And Jesus went about all Galilee, teaching in their synagogues, preaching the gospel of the kingdom, and healing all kinds of sickness and all kinds of disease among the people.

24 *Then His fame went throughout all Syria; and they brought to Him all sick people who were afflicted with various diseases and torments, and those who were demon-possessed, epileptics, and paralytics; and He healed them.*

25 *Great multitudes followed Him—from Galilee, and from Decapolis, Jerusalem, Judea, and beyond the Jordan.*

1) How is John the Baptist described in Matthew's gospel?

_____

_____

_____

_____

2) What happened at the baptism of Christ?

_____

_____

_____

_____

3) In what ways did Satan seek to tempt Christ, and how did Jesus respond?

_____

_____

_____

_____

_____

4) What features marked the beginning of Christ's ministry?

_____

_____

_____

_____

_____

GOING DEEPER

Read Genesis 3:1–7 to see the first temptation in the Garden of Eden.

1 *Now the serpent was more cunning than any beast of the field which the LORD God had made. And he said to the woman, "Has God indeed said, 'You shall not eat of every tree of the garden'?"*

2 *And the woman said to the serpent, "We may eat the fruit of the trees of the garden;*

3 *but of the fruit of the tree which is in the midst of the garden, God has said, 'You shall not eat it, nor shall you touch it, lest you die.' "*

4 *Then the serpent said to the woman, "You will not surely die.*

5 *For God knows that in the day you eat of it your eyes will be opened, and you will be like God, knowing good and evil."*

6 *So when the woman saw that the tree was good for food, that it was pleasant to the eyes, and a tree desirable to make one wise, she took of its fruit and ate. She also gave to her husband with her, and he ate.*

7 *Then the eyes of both of them were opened, and they knew that they were naked; and they sewed fig leaves together and made themselves coverings.*

EXPLORING THE MEANING

5) Compare the first temptation of Adam and Eve with Christ's temptation. What common threads do you see? (See also 1 John 2:15–17.)

_____

_____

_____

_____

_____

6) Both John and Jesus preached a succinct message: "Repent!" What does this term really mean? What does it look like when a person truly repents?

_____

_____

_____

_____

_____

7) Why was it necessary for Jesus to be baptized? What was the significance of this act?

_____

_____

_____

_____

8) In what ways is Christ our role model for resisting temptation? What are the lessons we can learn from him?

_____

_____

_____

_____

9) Christ urged Simon, Peter, James, and John to follow him. What does "following Christ" look like today, twenty centuries later?

_____

_____

_____

_____

TRUTH FOR TODAY

Jesus has been there before us; He has met the worst Satan can give and has been victorious. More than that, He is eager to share that victory with His own people when they are tempted. "No temptation has overtaken you except such as is common to man; but God is faithful, who will not allow you to be tempted beyond what you are able, but with the temptation will also make the way of escape, that you may be able to bear it" (1 Cor. 10:13 NKJV).

We can have victory over temptation only by resisting in the way that Jesus resisted—by holding with complete obedience to God and His Word. Jesus endured temptation to the very limit of Satan's power, and He resisted to that very limit. He did not in the least degree allow temptation to develop into desire, much less into sin (James 1:13–15). He did not think the matter over or give it any consideration. He simply stood firmly in His Father's will and said no!

We find help against temptation, just as we find help for everything else in the Christian life, by "looking unto Jesus, the author and finisher of our faith" (Heb. 12:2 NKJV). A hurdler soon learns that if he looks at the hurdles as he runs, he will trip and fall. From start to finish he looks only at the goal, and by doing this, he clears the hurdles as they come. Keeping our eyes on our Lord Jesus Christ is our only hope of conquering temptation and faithfully running "with endurance the race that is set before us" (Heb. 12:1 NKJV).

REFLECTING ON THE TEXT

10) In these chapters we have seen Jesus resist all inducements to sin, and we have heard him tell sinners to turn away from evil. In what specific ways are you challenged by Matthew 3 and 4? What actions need to change in your life?

_____

_____

_____

_____

11) Write down your "escape plan" for the next time you face your most recurrent temptation. What exactly will you do to resist?

_____

_____

_____

_____

PERSONAL RESPONSE

Write out additional reflections, questions you may have, or a prayer.

3

THE MESSAGE OF THE KINGDOM
Matthew 5:1–7:29

DRAWING NEAR

A large part of Jesus' ministry was his preaching and teaching. Think about one of the best sermons or messages you've ever heard. Why does it stick out in your mind? What made it so powerful and memorable?

_____

_____

_____

_____

_____

THE CONTEXT

Until this point in Matthew, Jesus' words have been limited and reference to His teachings have been general. Now in one powerfully comprehensive yet compact message, the Lord sets forth the foundational truths of the gospel of the kingdom He came to proclaim. This one continuous message of the Lord found in Matthew 5–7 has traditionally been called the Sermon on the Mount. This teaching was delivered at one specific time. As we will see, these were revolutionary truths to the minds of those Jewish religionists who heard them. Christ's pronouncements have continued to explode with great impact on the minds of readers for over two thousand years.

Here is the manifesto of the new Monarch, who ushers in a new age with a new message about true righteousness. The underlying and overarching theme of Christ's sermon is that man has no righteousness of his own that can survive the scrutiny of God. On the contrary, salvation and blessing are offered freely by the grace of the King and must be received by faith.

Why is the Sermon on the Mount so important? Because it shows the absolute necessity of the new birth. God's perfect standards are much too high and demanding to be met by human power. Only those who partake of God's own nature through Jesus Christ can fulfill such demands. The sermon drives us to King Jesus as our only hope of meeting God's standards. Christ's revolutionary message also shows us God's pattern for true happiness and success.

Keys to the Text

Messiah and King: Most Jews of Jesus' day expected the Messiah, the "Anointed One," to be, first of all, a military and political leader who would deliver them from the yoke of Rome and establish a prosperous Jewish kingdom that would lead the world. He would be greater than any king, leader, or prophet in their history. They saw Jesus as the anticipated leader of a great welfare state in which even their routine physical needs would be provided. But Jesus would not allow Himself to be mistaken for that sort of king. The thrust of the Sermon on the Mount is that the message and work of the King are, first and most important, *internal* and not external, spiritual and moral rather than physical and political. Here we find no politics or social reform. His concern is for what men *are*, because what they are determines what they do.

Unleashing the Text

Read 5:1–7:29, noting the key words and definitions next to the passage.

Matthew 5:1–7:29 (NKJV)

was seated (5:1)—the normal posture for rabbis while teaching

Blessed (v. 3)—literally, "happy, fortunate, blissful," i.e., the divinely bestowed well-being that belongs only to the faithful

poor in spirit (v. 3)—the opposite of self-sufficiency, i.e., the deep humility of recognizing one's utter spiritual bankruptcy apart from God

theirs is the kingdom of heaven (v. 3)—Notice that the truth of salvation by grace is clearly presupposed in this opening verse of the Sermon on the Mount.

those who mourn (v. 4)—over sin, the godly sorrow that produces repentance leading to salvation without regret (2 Cor. 7:10)

the meek (v. 5)—the opposite of being out of control; not weakness, but supreme self-control empowered by the Spirit (see Gal. 5:23)

1 And seeing the multitudes, He went up on a mountain, and when He was seated His disciples came to Him.

2 Then He opened His mouth and taught them, saying:

3 "Blessed are the poor in spirit, For theirs is the kingdom of heaven.

4 Blessed are those who mourn, For they shall be comforted.

5 Blessed are the meek, For they shall inherit the earth.

6 Blessed are those who hunger and thirst for righteousness, For they shall be filled.

7 Blessed are the merciful, For they shall obtain mercy.

8 Blessed are the pure in heart, For they shall see God.

9 Blessed are the peacemakers, For they shall be called sons of God.

10 Blessed are those who are persecuted for righteousness' sake, For theirs is the kingdom of heaven.

11 "Blessed are you when they revile and persecute you, and say all kinds of evil against you falsely for My sake.

12 *Rejoice and be exceedingly glad, for great is your reward in heaven, for so they persecuted the prophets who were before you.*

13 *"You are the salt of the earth; but if the salt loses its flavor, how shall it be seasoned? It is then good for nothing but to be thrown out and trampled underfoot by men.*

14 *"You are the light of the world. A city that is set on a hill cannot be hidden.*

15 *Nor do they light a lamp and put it under a basket, but on a lampstand, and it gives light to all who are in the house.*

16 *Let your light so shine before men, that they may see your good works and glorify your Father in heaven.*

17 *"Do not think that I came to destroy the Law or the Prophets. I did not come to destroy but to fulfill.*

18 *For assuredly, I say to you, till heaven and earth pass away, one jot or one tittle will by no means pass from the law till all is fulfilled.*

19 *Whoever therefore breaks one of the least of these commandments, and teaches men so, shall be called least in the kingdom of heaven; but whoever does and teaches them, he shall be called great in the kingdom of heaven.*

20 *For I say to you, that unless your righteousness exceeds the righteousness of the scribes and Pharisees, you will by no means enter the kingdom of heaven.*

21 *"You have heard that it was said to those of old, 'You shall not murder, and whoever murders will be in danger of the judgment.'*

22 *But I say to you that whoever is angry with his brother without a cause shall be in danger of the judgment. And whoever says to his brother, 'Raca!' shall be in danger of the council. But whoever says, 'You fool!' shall be in danger of hell fire.*

23 *Therefore if you bring your gift to the altar, and there remember that your brother has something against you,*

If the salt loses its flavor, how shall it be seasoned (v. 13)—The salt common in the Dead Sea area is contaminated with gypsum and other minerals and may have a flat taste or be ineffective as a preservative.

Do not think that I came to destroy the Law or the Prophets (v. 17)—Jesus was neither giving a new law nor modifying or abolishing the old, but rather explaining the true significance of the moral content of Moses' law and the rest of the Old Testament.

till heaven and earth pass away ... till all is fulfilled (v. 18)—an affirmation of the inspiration and the enduring authority of all Scripture

one jot or one tittle (v. 18)—A "jot" refers to the smallest Hebrew letter, the *yohd*, which is a meager stroke of the pen, like an accent mark or an apostrophe; the "tittle" is a tiny extension on a Hebrew letter, like the serif in modern typefaces.

You have heard . . . But I say to you (vv. 21–22)—Jesus was not altering the terms of the law in any of these passages, but correcting what they had "heard"—the rabbinical understanding of the law.

Raca! (v. 22)—literally, "Empty-headed!"

Hell (v. 22)—a reference to the Hinnom Valley, southwest of Jerusalem, which, in Jesus' day, was a garbage dump where fires burned continually and was thus an apt symbol of eternal fire

pluck it out and cast *it* from you (v. 29)—Jesus was not advocating self-mutilation (for this would not in fact cure lust, which is actually a problem of the heart); rather he was using graphic hyperbole to demonstrate the seriousness of sins of lust and evil desire.

except sexual immorality (v. 32)—Divorce was allowed in cases of adultery. Luke 16:18 must be understood in the light of this verse.

24 *leave your gift there before the altar, and go your way. First be reconciled to your brother, and then come and offer your gift.*

25 *Agree with your adversary quickly, while you are on the way with him, lest your adversary deliver you to the judge, the judge hand you over to the officer, and you be thrown into prison.*

26 *Assuredly, I say to you, you will by no means get out of there till you have paid the last penny.*

27 *"You have heard that it was said to those of old, 'You shall not commit adultery.'*

28 *But I say to you that whoever looks at a woman to lust for her has already committed adultery with her in his heart.*

29 *If your right eye causes you to sin, pluck it out and cast it from you; for it is more profitable for you that one of your members perish, than for your whole body to be cast into hell.*

30 *And if your right hand causes you to sin, cut it off and cast it from you; for it is more profitable for you that one of your members perish, than for your whole body to be cast into hell.*

31 *"Furthermore it has been said, 'Whoever divorces his wife, let him give her a certificate of divorce.'*

32 *But I say to you that whoever divorces his wife for any reason except sexual immorality causes her to commit adultery; and whoever marries a woman who is divorced commits adultery.*

33 *"Again you have heard that it was said to those of old, 'You shall not swear falsely, but shall perform your oaths to the Lord.'*

34 *But I say to you, do not swear at all: neither by heaven, for it is God's throne;*

35 *nor by the earth, for it is His footstool; nor by Jerusalem, for it is the city of the great King.*

36 *Nor shall you swear by your head, because you cannot make one hair white or black.*

37 *But let your 'Yes' be 'Yes,' and your 'No,' 'No.' For whatever is more than these is from the evil one.*

38 *"You have heard that it was said, 'An eye for an eye and a tooth for a tooth.'*

39 *But I tell you not to resist an evil person. But whoever slaps you on your right cheek, turn the other to him also.*

40 *If anyone wants to sue you and take away your tunic, let him have your cloak also.*

41 *And whoever compels you to go one mile, go with him two.*

42 *Give to him who asks you, and from him who wants to borrow from you do not turn away.*

43 *"You have heard that it was said, 'You shall love your neighbor and hate your enemy.'*

44 *But I say to you, love your enemies, bless those who curse you, do good to those who hate you, and pray for those who spitefully use you and persecute you,*

45 *that you may be sons of your Father in heaven; for He makes His sun rise on the evil and on the good, and sends rain on the just and on the unjust.*

46 *For if you love those who love you, what reward have you? Do not even the tax collectors do the same?*

47 *And if you greet your brethren only, what do you do more than others? Do not even the tax collectors do so?*

48 *Therefore you shall be perfect, just as your Father in heaven is perfect.*

6:1 *"Take heed that you do not do your charitable deeds before men, to be seen by them. Otherwise you have no reward from your Father in heaven.*

2 *Therefore, when you do a charitable deed, do not sound a trumpet before you as the hypocrites do in the synagogues and in the streets, that they may have glory from men. Assuredly, I say to you, they have their reward.*

3 *But when you do a charitable deed, do not let your left hand know what your right hand is doing,*

4 *that your charitable deed may be in secret; and your Father who sees in secret will Himself reward you openly.*

An eye for an eye (v. 38)—The law did establish this standard as a principle for limiting retribution to ensure that the punishment in civil cases fit the crime (Ex. 21:24; Lev. 24:20; Deut. 19:21).

tax collectors (v. 46)—disloyal Israelites hired by the Romans to tax other Jews for personal profit, symbols for the worst kind of people

you shall be perfect (v. 48)—Christ sums up what the law itself demanded, an unattainable standard.

hypocrites (6:2)—This word had its origins in Greek theater, describing a character who wore a mask.

In this manner (v. 9)—The brief, simple, yet comprehensive prayer is a model, not merely a liturgy.

do not lead us into temptation (v. 13)—Though God does not tempt men (James 1:13), He allows us to face trials and tests (see Luke 22:31–32); this petition reflects a Christian's desire to avoid the dangers of sin altogether.

neither will your Father forgive your trespasses (v. 15)—not the withholding of a permanent and complete acquittal from the guilt and ultimate penalty of sin—this belongs to all who are in Christ; rather the withholding of day-to-day cleansing (1 John 1:9) that is necessary for intimacy with God

5 *"And when you pray, you shall not be like the hypocrites. For they love to pray standing in the synagogues and on the corners of the streets, that they may be seen by men. Assuredly, I say to you, they have their reward.*

6 *But you, when you pray, go into your room, and when you have shut your door, pray to your Father who is in the secret place; and your Father who sees in secret will reward you openly.*

7 *And when you pray, do not use vain repetitions as the heathen do. For they think that they will be heard for their many words.*

8 *"Therefore do not be like them. For your Father knows the things you have need of before you ask Him.*

9 *In this manner, therefore, pray: Our Father in heaven, Hallowed be Your name.*

10 *Your kingdom come. Your will be done On earth as it is in heaven.*

11 *Give us this day our daily bread.*

12 *And forgive us our debts, As we forgive our debtors.*

13 *And do not lead us into temptation, But deliver us from the evil one. For Yours is the kingdom and the power and the glory forever. Amen.*

14 *"For if you forgive men their trespasses, your heavenly Father will also forgive you.*

15 *But if you do not forgive men their trespasses, neither will your Father forgive your trespasses.*

16 *"Moreover, when you fast, do not be like the hypocrites, with a sad countenance. For they disfigure their faces that they may appear to men to be fasting. Assuredly, I say to you, they have their reward.*

17 *But you, when you fast, anoint your head and wash your face,*

18 *so that you do not appear to men to be fasting, but to your Father who is in the secret place; and your Father who sees in secret will reward you openly.*

19 *"Do not lay up for yourselves treasures on earth, where moth and rust destroy and where thieves break in and steal;*

20 *but lay up for yourselves treasures in heaven, where neither moth nor rust destroys and where thieves do not break in and steal.*

21 *For where your treasure is, there your heart will be also.*

22 *"The lamp of the body is the eye. If therefore your eye is good, your whole body will be full of light.*

23 *But if your eye is bad, your whole body will be full of darkness. If therefore the light that is in you is darkness, how great is that darkness!*

24 *"No one can serve two masters; for either he will hate the one and love the other, or else he will be loyal to the one and despise the other. You cannot serve God and mammon.*

mammon (v. 24)—earthly, material treasures, especially money

25 *"Therefore I say to you, do not worry about your life, what you will eat or what you will drink; nor about your body, what you will put on. Is not life more than food and the body more than clothing?*

26 *Look at the birds of the air, for they neither sow nor reap nor gather into barns; yet your heavenly Father feeds them. Are you not of more value than they?*

27 *Which of you by worrying can add one cubit to his stature?*

28 *"So why do you worry about clothing? Consider the lilies of the field, how they grow: they neither toil nor spin;*

29 *and yet I say to you that even Solomon in all his glory was not arrayed like one of these.*

30 *Now if God so clothes the grass of the field, which today is, and tomorrow is thrown into the oven, will He not much more clothe you, O you of little faith?*

31 *"Therefore do not worry, saying, 'What shall we eat?' or 'What shall we drink?' or 'What shall we wear?'*

32 *For after all these things the Gentiles seek. For your heavenly Father knows that you need all these things.*

33 *But seek first the kingdom of God and His righteousness, and all these things shall be added to you.*

34 *Therefore do not worry about tomorrow, for tomorrow will worry about its own things. Sufficient for the day is its own trouble.*

Judge not (7:1)—Harsh, hypocritical, self-righteous, or other kinds of unfair judgments are forbidden, not the discerning of distinctions between good and evil.

7:1 "Judge not, that you be not judged.

2 For with what judgment you judge, you will be judged; and with the measure you use, it will be measured back to you.

3 And why do you look at the speck in your brother's eye, but do not consider the plank in your own eye?

4 Or how can you say to your brother, 'Let me remove the speck from your eye'; and look, a plank is in your own eye?

5 Hypocrite! First remove the plank from your own eye, and then you will see clearly to remove the speck from your brother's eye.

6 "Do not give what is holy to the dogs; nor cast your pearls before swine, lest they trample them under their feet, and turn and tear you in pieces.

7 "Ask, and it will be given to you; seek, and you will find; knock, and it will be opened to you.

8 For everyone who asks receives, and he who seeks finds, and to him who knocks it will be opened.

9 Or what man is there among you who, if his son asks for bread, will give him a stone?

10 Or if he asks for a fish, will he give him a serpent?

you ... being evil (v. 11)—Jesus presupposes the doctrine of human depravity.

11 If you then, being evil, know how to give good gifts to your children, how much more will your Father who is in heaven give good things to those who ask Him!

12 Therefore, whatever you want men to do to you, do also to them, for this is the Law and the Prophets.

13 "Enter by the narrow gate; for wide is the gate and broad is the way that leads to destruction, and there are many who go in by it.

difficult is the way (v. 14)—Salvation is by grace alone, but is not easy.

14 Because narrow is the gate and difficult is the way which leads to life, and there are few who find it.

15 "Beware of false prophets, who come to you in sheep's clothing, but inwardly they are ravenous wolves.

16 You will know them by their fruits. Do men gather grapes from thornbushes or figs from thistles?

17 Even so, every good tree bears good fruit, but a bad tree bears bad fruit.

18 A good tree cannot bear bad fruit, nor can a bad tree bear good fruit.

19 *Every tree that does not bear good fruit is cut down and thrown into the fire.*

20 *Therefore by their fruits you will know them.*

21 *"Not everyone who says to Me, 'Lord, Lord,' shall enter the kingdom of heaven, but he who does the will of My Father in heaven.*

22 *Many will say to Me in that day, 'Lord, Lord, have we not prophesied in Your name, cast out demons in Your name, and done many wonders in Your name?'*

23 *And then I will declare to them, 'I never knew you; depart from Me, you who practice lawlessness!'*

24 *"Therefore whoever hears these sayings of Mine, and does them, I will liken him to a wise man who built his house on the rock:*

25 *and the rain descended, the floods came, and the winds blew and beat on that house; and it did not fall, for it was founded on the rock.*

26 *"But everyone who hears these sayings of Mine, and does not do them, will be like a foolish man who built his house on the sand:*

27 *and the rain descended, the floods came, and the winds blew and beat on that house; and it fell. And great was its fall."*

28 *And so it was, when Jesus had ended these sayings, that the people were astonished at His teaching,*

29 *for He taught them as one having authority, and not as the scribes.*

Not everyone who says . . . but he who does (v. 21)—The faith that says but does not do is really unbelief.

not as the scribes (v. 29)—Whereas the scribes quoted others to establish the authority of their teachings, Jesus was His own authority (28:18).

1) What is the central message of the Beatitudes (5:3–12)?

_____

_____

_____

2) How did Jesus differ from other teachers of His day in the way He handled the Scripture?

_____

_____

_____

3) Sum up Jesus' teaching in the Sermon on the Mount about prayer.

_____

_____

_____

_____

4) According to this message, how is a person made right with God? (Cite specific verses to support your answer.)

_____

_____

_____

_____

GOING DEEPER

Read Luke 6:20–31, sometimes called "the Sermon on the Plateau."

20 *Then He lifted up His eyes toward His disciples, and said: "Blessed are you poor, for yours is the kingdom of God.*

21 *Blessed are you who hunger now, for you shall be filled. Blessed are you who weep now, for you shall laugh.*

22 *Blessed are you when men hate you, and when they exclude you, and revile you, and cast out your name as evil, for the Son of Man's sake.*

23 *Rejoice in that day and leap for joy! For indeed your reward is great in heaven, for in like manner their fathers did to the prophets.*

24 *"But woe to you who are rich, for you have received your consolation.*

25 *Woe to you who are full, for you shall hunger. Woe to you who laugh now, for you shall mourn and weep.*

26 *Woe to you when all men speak well of you, for so did their fathers to the false prophets.*

27 *But I say to you who hear: Love your enemies, do good to those who hate you,*

28 *bless those who curse you, and pray for those who spitefully use you.*

29 *To him who strikes you on the one cheek, offer the other also. And from him who takes away your cloak, do not withhold your tunic either.*

30 *Give to everyone who asks of you. And from him who takes away your goods do not ask them back.*

31 *And just as you want men to do to you, you also do to them likewise.*

Exploring the Meaning

5) Compare and contrast the teaching in Luke with the Sermon on the Mount.

_____

_____

_____

6) What is the meaning of the word *blessed* as used by Christ?

_____

_____

7) Why would Jesus' interpretation of the Old Testament Scriptures regarding murder and adultery and divorce upset the religious leaders of the day?

_____

_____

8) What does Jesus mean in 5:48, "be perfect, just as your Father in heaven is perfect"? How are we to interpret this passage?

_____

_____

_____

Truth for Today

We can see at least five reasons that the Sermon on the Mount is important. First, it shows the absolute necessity of the new birth. Its standards are much too high and demanding to be met by human power. Only those who partake of God's own nature through Jesus Christ can fulfill such demands. The standards of the Sermon on the Mount go far beyond those of Moses in the Law, demanding not only righteous actions but righteous attitudes—not just that men *do* right but that they *be* right. No part of Scripture more clearly shows man's desperate situation without God.

Second, the sermon intends to drive the listener to Jesus Christ as man's only hope of meeting God's standards. If man cannot live up to the divine standard, he needs a supernatural power to enable him. The proper response to the sermon leads to Christ.

Third, the sermon gives God's pattern for happiness and for true success. It reveals the standards, the objectives, and the motivations that, with God's help, will fulfill what God has designed man to be. Here we find the way of joy, peace, and contentment.

Fourth, the sermon is perhaps the greatest scriptural resource for witnessing, or reaching others for Christ. A Christian who personifies these principles of Jesus will be a spiritual magnet, attracting others to the Lord who empowers him. The life that is obedient to the principles of the Sermon on the Mount is the church's greatest tool for evangelism.

Fifth, the life obedient to the maxims of this proclamation is the only life that is pleasing to God. That is the believer's highest reason for following Jesus' teaching—it pleases God.

REFLECTING ON THE TEXT

9) What surprises you most about Jesus' Sermon on the Mount? Why?

_____

_____

_____

10) What part of the sermon is most convicting to you? Why?

_____

_____

_____

11) How can you be a "doer of the Word" (James 1:22) now that you have studied Matthew 5–7? (Be specific!)

_____

_____

_____

PERSONAL RESPONSE

Write out additional reflections, questions you may have, or a prayer.

_____

_____

_____

_____

_____

4

THE POWER OF THE KING
Matthew 8:1–9:38

DRAWING NEAR

If you could personally witness any miracle that Jesus performed, which supernatural event would you pick, and why?

_____

_____

_____

THE CONTEXT

Matthew 8 begins where chapter 4 leaves off, with the Sermon on the Mount as a sort of parenthesis in between. At the end of chapter 4, Jesus was going about "all Galilee, teaching in their synagogues, preaching the gospel of the kingdom, and healing all kinds of sickness and all kinds of disease among the people" (v. 23 NKJV).

In establishing Jesus' messiahship, Matthew demonstrated Jesus' legal qualification through His genealogy, His prophetic qualification through the fulfillment of prophecy by His birth and infancy, His divine qualification by the Father's own attestation at His baptism, His spiritual qualification by His perfect resistance to Satan's temptations, and His theological qualification through the teaching of the Sermon on the Mount. Now in chapters 8 and 9 Matthew dramatically sets forth another qualification: Jesus' divine power. These two chapters are critical to understanding the life and ministry of Christ. Matthew's purpose in recording these miracles, like Jesus' purpose in performing them, was to confirm His deity and His claim to be the Messiah of Israel and the Savior of the world.

KEYS TO THE TEXT

Disease and Jesus' Healing: In New Testament times, disease was rampant, and medical science as we know it did not exist. If a person survived a serious disease, it was usually because the malady had run its course. Whether or not it was fatal, most disease caused great pain and suffering, for which there was little remedy. Sufferers were often left scarred, deformed, crippled, or otherwise debilitated for the rest of their lives. Plagues would sometimes wipe out entire villages, cities, or even regions. The list of diseases was long, and life expectancy was short. Many diseases are mentioned in Scripture. We read of various forms of paralysis and atrophy, blindness, and deafness. We are told of boils, infected glands, various forms of edema, dysentery, mutism and other speech disorders, epilepsy, intestinal disorders, and many unidentified diseases.

When Jesus healed, He did so with a word or a touch, without gimmicks, formulas, or fanfare. He healed instantaneously, with no drawn-out period of waiting or of gradual restoration. He healed totally, not partially, no matter how serious the disease or deformity. He healed everyone who came to Him and even some who never saw Him. He healed organic as well as functional afflictions. Most dramatically and powerfully of all, He even raised the dead.

Unleashing the Text

Read 8:1–9:38, noting the key words and definitions next to the passage.

Matthew 8:1–9:38 (NKJV)

1 *When He had come down from the mountain, great multitudes followed Him.*

if You are willing (8:2)—He had no doubt about Christ's power, only His will (see Mark 1:40–45).

2 *And behold, a leper came and worshiped Him, saying, "Lord, if You are willing, You can make me clean."*

3 *Then Jesus put out His hand and touched him, saying, "I am willing; be cleansed." Immediately his leprosy was cleansed.*

4 *And Jesus said to him, "See that you tell no one; but go your way, show yourself to the priest, and offer the gift that Moses commanded, as a testimony to them."*

tell no one (v. 4)—Christ did not want publicity over such miracles to hinder His mission and divert public attention from His message.

centurion (v. 5)—a Roman military officer who commanded (see v. 9) one hundred men

5 *Now when Jesus had entered Capernaum, a centurion came to Him, pleading with Him,*

6 *saying, "Lord, my servant is lying at home paralyzed, dreadfully tormented."*

7 *And Jesus said to him, "I will come and heal him."*

8 *The centurion answered and said, "Lord, I am not worthy that You should come under my roof. But only speak a word, and my servant will be healed.*

9 *For I also am a man under authority, having soldiers under me. And I say to this one, 'Go,' and he goes; and to another, 'Come,' and he comes; and to my servant, 'Do this,' and he does it."*

10 *When Jesus heard it, He marveled, and said to those who followed, "Assuredly, I say to you, I have not found such great faith, not even in Israel!*

11 *And I say to you that many will come from east and west, and sit down with Abraham, Isaac, and Jacob in the kingdom of heaven.*

12 *But the sons of the kingdom will be cast out into outer darkness. There will be weeping and gnashing of teeth."*

13 *Then Jesus said to the centurion, "Go your way; and as you have believed, so let it be done for you." And his servant was healed that same hour.*

14 *Now when Jesus had come into Peter's house, He saw his wife's mother lying sick with a fever.*

15 *So He touched her hand, and the fever left her. And she arose and served them.*

16 *When evening had come, they brought to Him many who were demon-possessed. And He cast out the spirits with a word, and healed all who were sick,*

17 *that it might be fulfilled which was spoken by Isaiah the prophet, saying: "He Himself took our infirmities And bore our sicknesses."*

18 *And when Jesus saw great multitudes about Him, He gave a command to depart to the other side.*

19 *Then a certain scribe came and said to Him, "Teacher, I will follow You wherever You go."*

20 *And Jesus said to him, "Foxes have holes and birds of the air have nests, but the Son of Man has nowhere to lay His head."*

21 *Then another of His disciples said to Him, "Lord, let me first go and bury my father."*

22 *But Jesus said to him, "Follow Me, and let the dead bury their own dead."*

23 *Now when He got into a boat, His disciples followed Him.*

24 *And suddenly a great tempest arose on the sea, so that the boat was covered with the waves. But He was asleep.*

I have not found such great faith, not even in Israel! (v. 10)—The centurion understood Jesus' absolute authority (vv. 8–9) as not even some of Jesus' own disciples did.

weeping and gnashing (v. 12)—descriptive of the eternal agonies of those in hell

demon-possessed (v. 16)—means "demonized," or under the internal control of a demon

a certain scribe (v. 19)—This man was breaking with his fellow scribes by publicly declaring his willingness to follow Jesus, but Jesus knew that he had not counted the cost in terms of suffering and inconvenience.

Son of Man (v. 20)—The messianic title Jesus used for Himself more than any other, occurring eighty-three times in the Gospels, always by Jesus Himself.

let me first go and bury my father (v. 21)—a common figure of speech meaning, "Let me wait until I receive my inheritance."

suddenly a great tempest arose (v. 24)—Since the Sea of Galilee is more than 690 feet below sea level and surrounded by mountains and hills, strong winds often sweep through the narrow surrounding gorges into this valley, causing extremely sudden and violent storms.

the winds and the sea obey Him (v. 27)—convincing proof of His deity

25 *Then His disciples came to Him and awoke Him, saying, "Lord, save us! We are perishing!"*

26 *But He said to them, "Why are you fearful, O you of little faith?" Then He arose and rebuked the winds and the sea, and there was a great calm.*

27 *So the men marveled, saying, "Who can this be, that even the winds and the sea obey Him?"*

28 *When He had come to the other side, to the country of the Gergesenes, there met Him two demon-possessed men, coming out of the tombs, exceedingly fierce, so that no one could pass that way.*

29 *And suddenly they cried out, saying, "What have we to do with You, Jesus, You Son of God? Have You come here to torment us before the time?"*

30 *Now a good way off from them there was a herd of many swine feeding.*

31 *So the demons begged Him, saying, "If You cast us out, permit us to go away into the herd of swine."*

32 *And He said to them, "Go." So when they had come out, they went into the herd of swine. And suddenly the whole herd of swine ran violently down the steep place into the sea, and perished in the water.*

begged Him to depart (v. 34)—perhaps out of concern over the financial impact from the loss of the pigs, or fear at being in the presence of such spiritual power

33 *Then those who kept them fled; and they went away into the city and told everything, including what had happened to the demon-possessed men.*

34 *And behold, the whole city came out to meet Jesus. And when they saw Him, they begged Him to depart from their region.*

9:1 *So He got into a boat, crossed over, and came to His own city.*

2 *Then behold, they brought to Him a paralytic lying on a bed. When Jesus saw their faith, He said to the paralytic, "Son, be of good cheer; your sins are forgiven you."*

3 *And at once some of the scribes said within themselves, "This Man blasphemes!"*

knowing their thoughts (v. 4)— Though Jesus humbled Himself (Phil. 2:4–8) and set aside the independent use of His divine prerogatives in incarnation (John 5:30), He was still fully God and, therefore, omniscient.

4 *But Jesus, knowing their thoughts, said, "Why do you think evil in your hearts?*

5 For which is easier, to say, 'Your sins are forgiven you,' or to say, 'Arise and walk'?

6 But that you may know that the Son of Man has power on earth to forgive sins"—then He said to the paralytic, "Arise, take up your bed, and go to your house."

7 And he arose and departed to his house.

8 Now when the multitudes saw it, they marveled and glorified God, who had given such power to men.

9 As Jesus passed on from there, He saw a man named Matthew sitting at the tax office. And He said to him, "Follow Me." So he arose and followed Him.

10 Now it happened, as Jesus sat at the table in the house, that behold, many tax collectors and sinners came and sat down with Him and His disciples.

11 And when the Pharisees saw it, they said to His disciples, "Why does your Teacher eat with tax collectors and sinners?"

12 When Jesus heard that, He said to them, "Those who are well have no need of a physician, but those who are sick.

13 But go and learn what this means: 'I desire mercy and not sacrifice.' For I did not come to call the righteous, but sinners, to repentance."

14 Then the disciples of John came to Him, saying, "Why do we and the Pharisees fast often, but Your disciples do not fast?"

15 And Jesus said to them, "Can the friends of the bridegroom mourn as long as the bridegroom is with them? But the days will come when the bridegroom will be taken away from them, and then they will fast.

16 No one puts a piece of unshrunk cloth on an old garment; for the patch pulls away from the garment, and the tear is made worse.

17 Nor do they put new wine into old wineskins, or else the wineskins break, the wine is spilled, and the wineskins are ruined. But they put new wine into new wineskins, and both are preserved."

which is easier (v. 5)—It is certainly easier to claim the power to pronounce absolution from sin than to demonstrate the power to heal, but Christ actually proved His power to forgive by instantly healing the man of his paralysis.

well . . . sick (v. 12)—The Pharisees thought they were well—religiously pure and whole; the outcasts knew they were not. Salvation can't come to the self-righteous.

then they will fast (v. 15)—Using the analogy of a wedding party, Jesus answered that as long as Christ was present with them, there was too much joy for fasting.

unshrunk cloth on an old garment (v. 16)—That new cloth does not work on old material is analogous to trying to patch New Covenant truth onto old Mosaic ceremonial forms.

a flow of blood for twelve years (v. 20)—This woman's serious physical affliction also left her permanently unclean for ceremonial reasons, and shunned by all.

the hem of His garment (v. 20)—probably one of the tassels that were sown to the corners of a garment in order to remind the wearer to obey God's commandments

sleeping (v. 24)—Sleep is a designation for death in the New Testament.

18 While He spoke these things to them, behold, a ruler came and worshiped Him, saying, "My daughter has just died, but come and lay Your hand on her and she will live."

19 So Jesus arose and followed him, and so did His disciples.

20 And suddenly, a woman who had a flow of blood for twelve years came from behind and touched the hem of His garment.

21 For she said to herself, "If only I may touch His garment, I shall be made well."

22 But Jesus turned around, and when He saw her He said, "Be of good cheer, daughter; your faith has made you well." And the woman was made well from that hour.

23 When Jesus came into the ruler's house, and saw the flute players and the noisy crowd wailing,

24 He said to them, "Make room, for the girl is not dead, but sleeping." And they ridiculed Him.

25 But when the crowd was put outside, He went in and took her by the hand, and the girl arose.

26 And the report of this went out into all that land.

27 When Jesus departed from there, two blind men followed Him, crying out and saying, "Son of David, have mercy on us!"

28 And when He had come into the house, the blind men came to Him. And Jesus said to them, "Do you believe that I am able to do this?" They said to Him, "Yes, Lord."

29 Then He touched their eyes, saying, "According to your faith let it be to you."

30 And their eyes were opened. And Jesus sternly warned them, saying, "See that no one knows it."

31 But when they had departed, they spread the news about Him in all that country.

32 As they went out, behold, they brought to Him a man, mute and demon-possessed.

33 And when the demon was cast out, the mute spoke. And the multitudes marveled, saying, "It was never seen like this in Israel!"

34 But the Pharisees said, "He casts out demons by the ruler of the demons."

35 Then Jesus went about all the cities and villages, teaching in their synagogues, preaching the gospel of the kingdom, and healing every sickness and every disease among the people.

36 But when He saw the multitudes, He was moved with compassion for them, because they were weary and scattered, like sheep having no shepherd.

37 Then He said to His disciples, "The harvest truly is plentiful, but the laborers are few.

38 Therefore pray the Lord of the harvest to send out laborers into His harvest."

every sickness and every disease (v. 35)—an unprecedented healing display, giving impressive evidence of His deity and making the Jews' rejection all the more heinous

1) How many different kinds of illnesses do you count in Matthew 8–9? Identify the different types of miracles Jesus performed.

2) With what attitude and beliefs did the centurion approach Jesus (8:5–13)?

3) How did Jesus respond to the large crowds who were clamoring for His blessings (8:18–22)?

4) Where was Matthew when Jesus called him to follow (9:9)?

_____

_____

_____

_____

5) The Pharisees begin to notice Jesus. What was their complaint (9:10–13)?

_____

_____

_____

_____

6) What do you learn about Jesus from His words and actions? What was His mission and purpose?

_____

_____

_____

_____

GOING DEEPER

Luke 5:17–39 gives us another "window" into many of these same incidents. Read that passage and see what extra insights you can glean.

17 *Now it happened on a certain day, as He was teaching, that there were Pharisees and teachers of the law sitting by, who had come out of every town of Galilee, Judea, and Jerusalem. And the power of the Lord was present to heal them.*

18 *Then behold, men brought on a bed a man who was paralyzed, whom they sought to bring in and lay before Him.*

19 *And when they could not find how they might bring him in, because of the crowd, they went up on the housetop and let him down with his bed through the tiling into the midst before Jesus.*

20 *When He saw their faith, He said to him, "Man, your sins are forgiven you."*

21 *And the scribes and the Pharisees began to reason, saying, "Who is this who speaks blasphemies? Who can forgive sins but God alone?"*

22 *But when Jesus perceived their thoughts, He answered and said to them, "Why are you reasoning in your hearts?*

23 *Which is easier, to say, 'Your sins are forgiven you,' or to say, 'Rise up and walk'?*

24 *But that you may know that the Son of Man has power on earth to forgive sins"—He said to the man who was paralyzed, "I say to you, arise, take up your bed, and go to your house."*

25 *Immediately he rose up before them, took up what he had been lying on, and departed to his own house, glorifying God.*

26 *And they were all amazed, and they glorified God and were filled with fear, saying, "We have seen strange things today!"*

27 *After these things He went out and saw a tax collector named Levi, sitting at the tax office. And He said to him, "Follow Me."*

28 *So he left all, rose up, and followed Him.*

29 *Then Levi gave Him a great feast in his own house. And there were a great number of tax collectors and others who sat down with them.*

30 *And their scribes and the Pharisees complained against His disciples, saying, "Why do You eat and drink with tax collectors and sinners?"*

31 *Jesus answered and said to them, "Those who are well have no need of a physician, but those who are sick.*

32 *I have not come to call the righteous, but sinners, to repentance."*

33 *Then they said to Him, "Why do the disciples of John fast often and make prayers, and likewise those of the Pharisees, but Yours eat and drink?"*

34 *And He said to them, "Can you make the friends of the bridegroom fast while the bridegroom is with them?*

35 *But the days will come when the bridegroom will be taken away from them; then they will fast in those days."*

36 *Then He spoke a parable to them: "No one puts a piece from a new garment on an old one; otherwise the new makes a tear, and also the piece that was taken out of the new does not match the old.*

37 *And no one puts new wine into old wineskins; or else the new wine will burst the wineskins and be spilled, and the wineskins will be ruined.*

38 *But new wine must be put into new wineskins, and both are preserved.*

39 *And no one, having drunk old wine, immediately desires new; for he says, 'The old is better.' "*

EXPLORING THE MEANING

7) Why did Jesus heal the paralytic? What was the result?

_____

_____

_____

_____

8) Why do you think Jesus commanded many of the people he healed not to tell anyone? Why did He seemingly "discourage" would-be followers with demanding words of discipleship?

_____

_____

_____

_____

9) Put yourself in the boat with the disciples in the midst of the storm. You wake Jesus up, and He calms the wind and the waves. How do you feel? What conclusions would you draw?

_____

_____

_____

_____

10) Why do you think the Gergesenes (or Gadarenes, as some translations refer to them) urged Jesus to leave their region?

_____

_____

_____

11) What do you learn from Matthew 8–9 about what it means to be Jesus' disciple?

_____

_____

_____

Truth for Today

It is small wonder that Jesus' healing miracles brought such immediate and widespread attention. For people who seldom had means to alleviate even the symptoms of disease, the prospect of complete cure was almost too astounding to be believed. Even the rumor of such a thing would bring a multitude of the curious and hopeful. For those of us who live in a society where basic good health is accepted largely as a matter of course, it is difficult to appreciate the impact Jesus' healing ministry had in Palestine. For a brief period of time, disease and other physical afflictions were virtually eliminated as Jesus went through the land, healing thousands.

Jesus Himself said on several occasions that His miraculous works alone should have been more than enough reason to believe in Him (John 10:38; 14:11). Such things had never happened before in the history of the world and could only have a divine cause. That is what made the rejection of the scribes, Pharisees, Sadducees, and others so self-condemnatory. No one could deny that Jesus performed the miracles, and only the most hard-hearted resistance to the truth could make a person reject His divinity in the face of such overpowering evidence. Those who would not believe in Jesus were indicted by every miracle He performed.

Reflecting on the Text

12) Many Christians have heard about Jesus' teaching and miracles all their lives. How can we who are so familiar with the Gospel accounts regain a sense of wonder at Christ's power?

_____

_____

_____

_____

_____

13) How might God receive the glory from a person who is never healed?

_____

_____

_____

_____

14) Where specifically in your life do you desperately need to trust in the power of God? How can you demonstrate that trust today?

_____

_____

_____

_____

PERSONAL RESPONSE

Write out additional reflections, questions you may have, or a prayer.

_____

_____

_____

_____

_____

_____

_____

_____

_____

_____

_____

_____

_____

_____

5

ALL THE KING'S MEN
Matthew 10:1–42

DRAWING NEAR

Jesus prayerfully chose twelve good men to be His followers and form the foundation for the church. If you had to pick people to plant a new church, what kinds of people would be advantageous to have on your team? What kinds of personalities might be an impediment?

_____

_____

_____

THE CONTEXT

It is encouraging to realize that Jesus did not call the twelve disciples (who became apostles) on the basis of their innate worthiness or personal capabilities or faithfulness, but solely on the basis of what He could make of them by His own power working through them. During the disciples' three years of training under Jesus, we see few signs of maturity and reliability but many signs of pettiness and inadequacy. It is a marvelous insight into the grace of God toward us to see Christ deal so lovingly and patiently with men who are so weak and unresponsive.

Following the list of the men the King selected, Matthew records Christ's words about the basic task of ministry, some warnings about how their ministry will be received, and some concluding remarks about the cost of ministry.

KEYS TO THE TEXT

Workers for the Harvest: Notice that Jesus called His disciples to pray for workers (see 9:38), and then He called *them* to become workers. As they began to see the world as Christ sees it, looking out on lost humanity through their Lord's eyes and with His heart of compassion, they also began to see that they themselves were called to go out and invite the lost into the Lord's kingdom. Vital as it is, prayer is not all that is required. The believer who prays for God to send workers, but is unwilling to go himself, prays insincerely and hypocritically. The Christian who genuinely prays for God to send witnesses is also willing to be a witness.

UNLEASHING THE TEXT

Read 10:1–42, noting the key words and definitions next to the passage.

disciples...apostles (10:1)—*Disciple* means "student," one who is taught by another; *apostles* refers to qualified representatives who are sent on a mission.

the names of the twelve apostles (v. 2)—The Twelve are always listed in a similar order (see Mark 3:16–19; Luke 6:13–16; Acts 1:13). Peter is always named first; Judas Iscariot is always named last.

James the *son* of Alphaeus (v. 4)—Four men in the New Testament are named James: (1) the apostle James, brother of John; (2) the disciple mentioned here, also called "James the Less" (Mark 15:40); (3) James, father of Judas (not Iscariot, Luke 6:16); and (4) James, the Lord's half-brother (Gal. 1:19; Mark 6:3), who wrote the epistle that bears the name and played a leading role in the early Jerusalem church (Acts 12:17; 15:13; Gal. 1:19).

Do not go into the way of the Gentiles (v. 5)—Christ did not forbid His disciples to preach to Gentiles or Samaritans if they encountered them on the way, but they were to take the message first to the covenant people, in the regions nearby.

Freely you have received, freely give (v. 8)—Jesus forbade them to charge money for their ministry but permitted them to accept support to meet their basic needs.

peace (v. 13)—equivalent to the Hebrew "shalom" and refers to prosperity, well-being, or blessing

shake off the dust from your feet (v. 14)—It was common for Jews to shake the dust off their feet as an expression of disdain when returning from Gentile regions.

Matthew 10:1–42 (NKJV)

1 And when He had called His twelve disciples to Him, He gave them power over unclean spirits, to cast them out, and to heal all kinds of sickness and all kinds of disease.

2 Now the names of the twelve apostles are these: first, Simon, who is called Peter, and Andrew his brother; James the son of Zebedee, and John his brother;

3 Philip and Bartholomew; Thomas and Matthew the tax collector; James the son of Alphaeus, and Lebbaeus, whose surname was Thaddaeus;

4 Simon the Cananite, and Judas Iscariot, who also betrayed Him.

5 These twelve Jesus sent out and commanded them, saying: "Do not go into the way of the Gentiles, and do not enter a city of the Samaritans.

6 But go rather to the lost sheep of the house of Israel.

7 And as you go, preach, saying, 'The kingdom of heaven is at hand.'

8 Heal the sick, cleanse the lepers, raise the dead, cast out demons. Freely you have received, freely give.

9 Provide neither gold nor silver nor copper in your money belts,

10 nor bag for your journey, nor two tunics, nor sandals, nor staffs; for a worker is worthy of his food.

11 "Now whatever city or town you enter, inquire who in it is worthy, and stay there till you go out.

12 And when you go into a household, greet it.

13 If the household is worthy, let your peace come upon it. But if it is not worthy, let your peace return to you.

14 And whoever will not receive you nor hear your words, when you depart from that house or city, shake off the dust from your feet.

15 *Assuredly, I say to you, it will be more tolerable for the land of Sodom and Gomorrah in the day of judgment than for that city!*

16 *"Behold, I send you out as sheep in the midst of wolves. Therefore be wise as serpents and harmless as doves.*

17 *But beware of men, for they will deliver you up to councils and scourge you in their synagogues.*

deliver you up (v. 17)—a technical word, in this context; used for handing over a prisoner for punishment

18 *You will be brought before governors and kings for My sake, as a testimony to them and to the Gentiles.*

19 *But when they deliver you up, do not worry about how or what you should speak. For it will be given to you in that hour what you should speak;*

20 *for it is not you who speak, but the Spirit of your Father who speaks in you.*

21 *"Now brother will deliver up brother to death, and a father his child; and children will rise up against parents and cause them to be put to death.*

22 *And you will be hated by all for My name's sake. But he who endures to the end will be saved.*

23 *When they persecute you in this city, flee to another. For assuredly, I say to you, you will not have gone through the cities of Israel before the Son of Man comes.*

24 *"A disciple is not above his teacher, nor a servant above his master.*

not above (v. 24)—If the Teacher (Christ) suffers, so will His pupils. If they attack the Master (Christ) with blasphemies, so will they curse the servants.

25 *It is enough for a disciple that he be like his teacher, and a servant like his master. If they have called the master of the house Beelzebub, how much more will they call those of his household!*

Beelzebub (v. 25)—the Philistine deity associated with satanic idolatry, a later synonym for Satan

26 *Therefore do not fear them. For there is nothing covered that will not be revealed, and hidden that will not be known.*

27 *"Whatever I tell you in the dark, speak in the light; and what you hear in the ear, preach on the housetops.*

28 *And do not fear those who kill the body but cannot kill the soul. But rather fear Him who is able to destroy both soul and body in hell.*

fear Him (v. 28)—God is the one who destroys in hell; persecutors can only harm the body.

apart from your Father's will (v. 29)—Divine providence governs even the smallest details and even the most mundane matters.

29 Are not two sparrows sold for a copper coin? And not one of them falls to the ground apart from your Father's will.

30 But the very hairs of your head are all numbered.

31 Do not fear therefore; you are of more value than many sparrows.

32 "Therefore whoever confesses Me before men, him I will also confess before My Father who is in heaven.

33 But whoever denies Me before men, him I will also deny before My Father who is in heaven.

34 "Do not think that I came to bring peace on earth. I did not come to bring peace but a sword.

35 For I have come to 'set a man against his father, a daughter against her mother, and a daughter-in-law against her mother-in-law';

36 and 'a man's enemies will be those of his own household.'

37 He who loves father or mother more than Me is not worthy of Me. And he who loves son or daughter more than Me is not worthy of Me.

take his cross (v. 38)—a picture of a violent, degrading death and a demand for total commitment—even unto physical death

38 And he who does not take his cross and follow after Me is not worthy of Me.

39 He who finds his life will lose it, and he who loses his life for My sake will find it.

He who receives you receives Me (v. 40)—Christ lives in His people; therefore, how they are treated is how He is treated.

40 "He who receives you receives Me, and he who receives Me receives Him who sent Me.

41 He who receives a prophet in the name of a prophet shall receive a prophet's reward. And he who receives a righteous man in the name of a righteous man shall receive a righteous man's reward.

42 And whoever gives one of these little ones only a cup of cold water in the name of a disciple, assuredly, I say to you, he shall by no means lose his reward."

1) What were Jesus' instructions to the Twelve before sending them out?

_____

_____

_____

_____

_____

2) List the exciting and reassuring statements Jesus made to His disciples in this chapter.

_____

_____

_____

_____

_____

3) What troubling and faith-stretching predictions about their mission did Christ make?

_____

_____

_____

_____

4) What impresses you about the men Jesus chose to be His apprentices and representatives?

_____

_____

_____

_____

5) According to this passage, how does a servant of Christ act (vv. 32–42)?

_____

_____

_____

_____

_____

_____

GOING DEEPER

Jesus knew that His disciples' message to the house of Israel would not always be well received. The Old Testament prophets knew this all too well. Read Jeremiah 11:1–11, and note this prophet's experience of telling God's message.

1 *The word that came to Jeremiah from the LORD, saying,*

2 *"Hear the words of this covenant, and speak to the men of Judah and to the inhabitants of Jerusalem;*

3 *and say to them, 'Thus says the LORD God of Israel: "Cursed is the man who does not obey the words of this covenant*

4 *which I commanded your fathers in the day I brought them out of the land of Egypt, from the iron furnace, saying, 'Obey My voice, and do according to all that I command you; so shall you be My people, and I will be your God,'*

5 *that I may establish the oath which I have sworn to your fathers, to give them 'a land flowing with milk and honey,' as it is this day."' " And I answered and said, "So be it, LORD."*

6 *Then the LORD said to me, "Proclaim all these words in the cities of Judah and in the streets of Jerusalem, saying: 'Hear the words of this covenant and do them.*

7 *For I earnestly exhorted your fathers in the day I brought them up out of the land of Egypt, until this day, rising early and exhorting, saying, "Obey My voice."*

8 *Yet they did not obey or incline their ear, but everyone followed the dictates of his evil heart; therefore I will bring upon them all the words of this covenant, which I commanded them to do, but which they have not done.' "*

9 *And the LORD said to me, "A conspiracy has been found among the men of Judah and among the inhabitants of Jerusalem.*

10 *They have turned back to the iniquities of their forefathers who refused to hear My words, and they have gone after other gods to serve them; the house of Israel and the house of Judah have broken My covenant which I made with their fathers."*

11 *Therefore thus says the LORD: "Behold, I will surely bring calamity on them which they will not be able to escape; and though they cry out to Me, I will not listen to them."*

EXPLORING THE MEANING

6) How did Jeremiah's audience receive his God-ordained message? In what way was this similar to what the disciples' may have experienced on their mission?

_____

_____

_____

_____

7) In Matthew 10:16 Jesus used an analogy with four animals. What do these creatures symbolize, and what is the meaning of Jesus' words?

_____

_____

_____

_____

8) Why would someone knowingly follow Jesus when He promises hardship and persecution?

_____

_____

_____

_____

9) How would you summarize Matthew 10:38–39 in your own words?

_____

_____

_____

_____

_____

Truth for Today

The greatness of God's grace is seen in His choosing the undeserving to be His people and the unqualified to do His work. It should be a marvelous encouragement to every believer to know that the apostles had a nature like ours. Because there was no other way, God chose to bestow sanctifying grace on those who believe in His Son and by His own power to transform them into men and women of great usefulness. We are tempted to become discouraged and disheartened when our spiritual lives and witness suffer because of our sins and failures. Satan attempts to convince us that those shortcomings render us useless to God; but His using the apostles testifies to the opposite. They did not lead the church in turning the world upside down because they were extraordinarily talented or naturally gifted, but because—in spite of their human limitations and failures—they surrendered themselves to God, whose power is perfected in man's weakness (2 Cor. 12:9). Apart from the brief ministry of His own Son, the history of God's work on earth is the history of His using the unqualified.

Reflecting on the Text

10) How does your Christian experience compare with the rigorous standards set forth by Christ in Matthew 10?

_____

_____

_____

_____

_____

_____

11) In what ways have you personally seen Christ "bring a sword" (v. 34), turning family members against each other?

_____

_____

_____

_____

_____

12) How is your understanding of Jesus different as a result of Matthew 10? What changes do you plan to implement in your life and faith?

_____

_____

_____

_____

_____

PERSONAL RESPONSE

Write out additional reflections, questions you may have, or a prayer.

_____

_____

_____

_____

_____

_____

_____

_____

ADDITIONAL NOTES

_____

_____

_____

_____

_____

_____

_____

_____

_____

_____

_____

_____

_____

_____

_____

_____

_____

_____

_____

_____

_____

_____

_____

_____

6

THE REACTIONS TO THE KING
Matthew 11:1–12:50

DRAWING NEAR

There's no shortage of opinions about who Jesus is and no shortage of expressions for or against Him. What are some of the strongest reactions to Jesus—positive and negative—that you've heard or seen?

Why do you think Jesus elicits such strong reactions from people?

_____

_____

_____

_____

THE CONTEXT

The first ten chapters of Matthew are, in general, a series of testimonies that prove who Jesus is. Matthew marshals all of that evidence in the courtroom, as it were, to testify that Jesus is the Christ, the King of kings, the Son of God, and the Savior of the world. In chapters 11 and 12 Matthew focuses on the reactions of various individuals and groups to that evidence. Chapter 11 looks at the negative responses of doubt, criticism, and indifference, followed by a positive appeal to faith. Chapter 12 looks at the negative responses of rejection, amazement, blasphemy, and curious fascination, followed by another positive appeal to faith. The events of Matthew 12 mark a major turning point in Jesus' ministry, focusing on the rejection of His kingship by His own people. The mounting unbelief of Israel crystallizes into conscious rejection and a determination on the part of the nation's religious leaders to destroy Jesus.

KEYS TO THE TEXT

Pharisees: The Pharisees were a small (about 6,000), legalistic sect of the Jews who were known for their rigid adherence to the ceremonial fine points of the Law. Their name means "separated ones." Jesus rebuked them for using human tradition to nullify Scripture and for rank hypocrisy.

The Sabbath: Jewish tradition prohibited the practice of medicine on the Sabbath and doing labor for profit. But no actual law in the Old Testament forbade plucking grain for food, nor the giving of medicine, healing, or any other acts of mercy on the Sabbath. It is always lawful to do good. Christ has the prerogative to rule over not only man-made sabbatarian rules, but also over the Sabbath itself—which was designed for worshiping God. Again, this was an inescapable claim of deity—and as such it prompted the Pharisees' violent outrage.

Unleashing the Text

Read 11:1–12:50, noting the key words and definitions next to the passage.

Matthew 11:1–12:50 (NKJV)

1 *Now it came to pass, when Jesus finished commanding His twelve disciples, that He departed from there to teach and to preach in their cities.*

2 *And when John had heard in prison about the works of Christ, he sent two of his disciples*

Are You the Coming One, or do we look for another? (11:3)— John was confused by the turn of events: he was imprisoned, and Christ was carrying on a ministry of healing, not judgment, in Galilee, far from Jerusalem, the city of the King.

3 *and said to Him, "Are You the Coming One, or do we look for another?"*

4 *Jesus answered and said to them, "Go and tell John the things which you hear and see:*

5 *The blind see and the lame walk; the lepers are cleansed and the deaf hear; the dead are raised up and the poor have the gospel preached to them.*

6 *And blessed is he who is not offended because of Me."*

7 *As they departed, Jesus began to say to the multitudes concerning John: "What did you go out into the wilderness to see? A reed shaken by the wind?*

8 *But what did you go out to see? A man clothed in soft garments? Indeed, those who wear soft clothing are in kings' houses.*

9 *But what did you go out to see? A prophet? Yes, I say to you, and more than a prophet.*

10 *For this is he of whom it is written: 'Behold, I send My messenger before Your face, who will prepare Your way before You.'*

11 "Assuredly, I say to you, among those born of women there has not risen one greater than John the Baptist; but he who is least in the kingdom of heaven is greater than he.

12 And from the days of John the Baptist until now the kingdom of heaven suffers violence, and the violent take it by force.

13 For all the prophets and the law prophesied until John.

14 And if you are willing to receive it, he is Elijah who is to come.

15 He who has ears to hear, let him hear!

16 "But to what shall I liken this generation? It is like children sitting in the marketplaces and calling to their companions,

17 and saying: 'We played the flute for you, and you did not dance; we mourned to you, and you did not lament.'

18 For John came neither eating nor drinking, and they say, 'He has a demon.'

19 The Son of Man came eating and drinking, and they say, 'Look, a glutton and a winebibber, a friend of tax collectors and sinners!' But wisdom is justified by her children."

20 Then He began to rebuke the cities in which most of His mighty works had been done, because they did not repent:

21 "Woe to you, Chorazin! Woe to you, Bethsaida! For if the mighty works which were done in you had been done in Tyre and Sidon, they would have repented long ago in sackcloth and ashes.

22 But I say to you, it will be more tolerable for Tyre and Sidon in the day of judgment than for you.

23 And you, Capernaum, who are exalted to heaven, will be brought down to Hades; for if the mighty works which were done in you had been done in Sodom, it would have remained until this day.

24 But I say to you that it shall be more tolerable for the land of Sodom in the day of judgment than for you."

least . . . is greater than he (v. 11)—John was greater than the Old Testament prophets because he actually saw with his eyes and personally participated in the fulfillment of what they only prophesied, but all believers after the cross are greater still, because they participate in the full understanding and experience of something John merely foresaw in shadowy form—the actual atoning work of Christ.

the kingdom of heaven suffers violence (v. 12)—better rendered "The kingdom presses ahead relentlessly, and only the relentless press their way into it." Thus again Christ is magnifying the difficulty of entering the kingdom.

he is Elijah (v. 14)—I.e., he is the fulfillment of Malachi 4:5–6.

more tolerable (vv. 22, 24)—an indication that there will be degrees of punishment in hell for the ungodly

Capernaum . . . exalted . . . brought down (v. 23)—The sin of Capernaum—indifference to Christ—was worse than Sodom's gross wickedness.

25 *At that time Jesus answered and said, "I thank You, Father, Lord of heaven and earth, that You have hidden these things from the wise and prudent and have revealed them to babes.*

26 *Even so, Father, for so it seemed good in Your sight.*

27 *All things have been delivered to Me by My Father, and no one knows the Son except the Father. Nor does anyone know the Father except the Son, and the one to whom the Son wills to reveal Him.*

28 *Come to Me, all you who labor and are heavy laden, and I will give you rest.*

29 *Take My yoke upon you and learn from Me, for I am gentle and lowly in heart, and you will find rest for your souls.*

30 *For My yoke is easy and My burden is light."*

12:1 *At that time Jesus went through the grainfields on the Sabbath. And His disciples were hungry, and began to pluck heads of grain and to eat.*

2 *And when the Pharisees saw it, they said to Him, "Look, Your disciples are doing what is not lawful to do on the Sabbath!"*

3 *But He said to them, "Have you not read what David did when he was hungry, he and those who were with him:*

4 *how he entered the house of God and ate the showbread which was not lawful for him to eat, nor for those who were with him, but only for the priests?*

5 *Or have you not read in the law that on the Sabbath the priests in the temple profane the Sabbath, and are blameless?*

6 *Yet I say to you that in this place there is One greater than the temple.*

7 *But if you had known what this means, 'I desire mercy and not sacrifice,' you would not have condemned the guiltless.*

8 *For the Son of Man is Lord even of the Sabbath."*

9 *Now when He had departed from there, He went into their synagogue.*

Come to Me, all *you* who labor and are heavy laden (vv. 28–30)—An open invitation to all who hear, but phrased in such a way that the only ones who will respond to the invitation are those who are burdened by their own spiritual bankruptcy and the weight of trying to save themselves by keeping the Law.

not lawful to do on the Sabbath (12:2)—No law prohibited the plucking of grain in order to eat on the Sabbath; what was prohibited was labor for the sake of profit.

the showbread (v. 4)—the twelve consecrated loaves baked fresh each Sabbath and normally eaten by the priests only (Lev. 24:5–9)

greater than the temple (v. 6)—This is a straightforward claim of deity. The Lord Jesus was God incarnate—God dwelling in human flesh—far superior to a building that God merely visited.

the Son of Man is Lord even of the Sabbath (v. 8)—another inescapable claim of that deity prompted the Pharisees' violent outrage (v. 14)

10 *And behold, there was a man who had a withered hand. And they asked Him, saying, "Is it lawful to heal on the Sabbath?"—that they might accuse Him.*

11 *Then He said to them, "What man is there among you who has one sheep, and if it falls into a pit on the Sabbath, will not lay hold of it and lift it out?*

12 *Of how much more value then is a man than a sheep? Therefore it is lawful to do good on the Sabbath."*

13 *Then He said to the man, "Stretch out your hand." And he stretched it out, and it was restored as whole as the other.*

14 *Then the Pharisees went out and plotted against Him, how they might destroy Him.*

15 *But when Jesus knew it, He withdrew from there. And great multitudes followed Him, and He healed them all.*

16 *Yet He warned them not to make Him known,*

17 *that it might be fulfilled which was spoken by Isaiah the prophet, saying:*

18 *"Behold! My Servant whom I have chosen, My Beloved in whom My soul is well pleased! I will put My Spirit upon Him, and He will declare justice to the Gentiles.*

19 *He will not quarrel nor cry out, nor will anyone hear His voice in the streets.*

20 *A bruised reed He will not break, and smoking flax He will not quench, till He sends forth justice to victory;*

21 *And in His name Gentiles will trust."*

22 *Then one was brought to Him who was demon-possessed, blind and mute; and He healed him, so that the blind and mute man both spoke and saw.*

23 *And all the multitudes were amazed and said, "Could this be the Son of David?"*

24 *Now when the Pharisees heard it they said, "This fellow does not cast out demons except by Beelzebub, the ruler of the demons."*

warned them not to make Him known (v. 16)—Christ was concerned about the potential zealotry of those who would try to press Him into the conquering-hero mold that the rabbinical experts had made out of messianic prophecy.

bruised reed . . . smoking flax (v. 20)—The reed was used by shepherds to fashion a small musical instrument. Once cracked or worn, it was useless. A smoldering wick was also useless for giving light. These represent people who are deemed useless by the world. Christ's work was to restore and rekindle such people, not to "break" them or "quench" them.

kingdom of God has come (v. 28)—The King was in their midst, displaying His sovereign power by demonstrating His ability to bind Satan and his demons (v. 29).

the blasphemy *against* the Spirit (vv. 31–32)—No forgiveness was possible for these Pharisees who witnessed His miracles firsthand, knew the truth of His claims, and still ascribed His work to Satan.

every idle word (v. 36)—The most seemingly insignificant sin—even a slip of the tongue—carries the full potential of all hell's evil.

25 But Jesus knew their thoughts, and said to them: "Every kingdom divided against itself is brought to desolation, and every city or house divided against itself will not stand.

26 If Satan casts out Satan, he is divided against himself. How then will his kingdom stand?

27 And if I cast out demons by Beelzebub, by whom do your sons cast them out? Therefore they shall be your judges.

28 But if I cast out demons by the Spirit of God, surely the kingdom of God has come upon you.

29 Or how can one enter a strong man's house and plunder his goods, unless he first binds the strong man? And then he will plunder his house.

30 He who is not with Me is against Me, and he who does not gather with Me scatters abroad.

31 "Therefore I say to you, every sin and blasphemy will be forgiven men, but the blasphemy against the Spirit will not be forgiven men.

32 Anyone who speaks a word against the Son of Man, it will be forgiven him; but whoever speaks against the Holy Spirit, it will not be forgiven him, either in this age or in the age to come.

33 "Either make the tree good and its fruit good, or else make the tree bad and its fruit bad; for a tree is known by its fruit.

34 Brood of vipers! How can you, being evil, speak good things? For out of the abundance of the heart the mouth speaks.

35 A good man out of the good treasure of his heart brings forth good things, and an evil man out of the evil treasure brings forth evil things.

36 But I say to you that for every idle word men may speak, they will give account of it in the day of judgment.

37 For by your words you will be justified, and by your words you will be condemned."

38 Then some of the scribes and Pharisees answered, saying, "Teacher, we want to see a sign from You."

39 But He answered and said to them, "An evil and adulterous generation seeks after a sign, and no sign will be given to it except the sign of the prophet Jonah.

40 For as Jonah was three days and three nights in the belly of the great fish, so will the Son of Man be three days and three nights in the heart of the earth.

41 The men of Nineveh will rise up in the judgment with this generation and condemn it, because they repented at the preaching of Jonah; and indeed a greater than Jonah is here.

42 The queen of the South will rise up in the judgment with this generation and condemn it, for she came from the ends of the earth to hear the wisdom of Solomon; and indeed a greater than Solomon is here.

43 "When an unclean spirit goes out of a man, he goes through dry places, seeking rest, and finds none.

44 Then he says, 'I will return to my house from which I came.' And when he comes, he finds it empty, swept, and put in order.

45 Then he goes and takes with him seven other spirits more wicked than himself, and they enter and dwell there; and the last state of that man is worse than the first. So shall it also be with this wicked generation."

46 While He was still talking to the multitudes, behold, His mother and brothers stood outside, seeking to speak with Him.

47 Then one said to Him, "Look, Your mother and Your brothers are standing outside, seeking to speak with You."

48 But He answered and said to the one who told Him, "Who is My mother and who are My brothers?"

49 And He stretched out His hand toward His disciples and said, "Here are My mother and My brothers!

50 For whoever does the will of My Father in heaven is My brother and sister and mother."

An evil and adulterous generation (v. 39)—This speaks of unfaithfulness to God—spiritual adultery.

brothers (v. 46)—actual siblings (half-brothers) of Jesus

does the will of My Father (v. 50)—not salvation by works; doing the will of God is the evidence of salvation by grace

63

1) What do you learn about John the Baptist (11:1–18)?

_____

_____

_____

_____

2) What was the source of the conflicts between Jesus and the religious leaders in Matthew 12:1–13?

_____

_____

_____

_____

3) What does the prophecy of 12:18–21 say about Messiah?

_____

_____

_____

_____

4) What conclusions did the Pharisees make about Christ, based on His words and works?

_____

_____

_____

_____

5) How did Jesus respond when the scribes and Pharisees asked Him for an additional sign?

_____

_____

_____

_____

Going Deeper

Read Luke 11:17–32 for more insight about the Jewish leaders' rejection of Jesus.

17 *But He, knowing their thoughts, said to them: "Every kingdom divided against itself is brought to desolation, and a house divided against a house falls.*

18 *If Satan also is divided against himself, how will his kingdom stand? Because you say I cast out demons by Beelzebub.*

19 *And if I cast out demons by Beelzebub, by whom do your sons cast them out? Therefore they will be your judges.*

20 *But if I cast out demons with the finger of God, surely the kingdom of God has come upon you.*

21 *When a strong man, fully armed, guards his own palace, his goods are in peace.*

22 *But when a stronger than he comes upon him and overcomes him, he takes from him all his armor in which he trusted, and divides his spoils.*

23 *He who is not with Me is against Me, and he who does not gather with Me scatters.*

24 *"When an unclean spirit goes out of a man, he goes through dry places, seeking rest; and finding none, he says, 'I will return to my house from which I came.'*

25 *And when he comes, he finds it swept and put in order.*

26 *Then he goes and takes with him seven other spirits more wicked than himself, and they enter and dwell there; and the last state of that man is worse than the first."*

27 *And it happened, as He spoke these things, that a certain woman from the crowd raised her voice and said to Him, "Blessed is the womb that bore You, and the breasts which nursed You!"*

28 *But He said, "More than that, blessed are those who hear the word of God and keep it!"*

29 *And while the crowds were thickly gathered together, He began to say, "This is an evil generation. It seeks a sign, and no sign will be given to it except the sign of Jonah the prophet.*

30 *For as Jonah became a sign to the Ninevites, so also the Son of Man will be to this generation.*

31 *The queen of the South will rise up in the judgment with the men of this generation and condemn them, for she came from the ends of the earth to hear the wisdom of Solomon; and indeed a greater than Solomon is here.*

32 *The men of Nineveh will rise up in the judgment with this generation and condemn it, for they repented at the preaching of Jonah; and indeed a greater than Jonah is here.*

Exploring the Meaning

6) What was behind the Pharisees' intense hostility to Jesus?

_____

_____

_____

_____

7) According to Jesus, what is the unpardonable sin?

_____

_____

_____

_____

8) What are we to make of the religious leaders' request in Matthew 12:38?

_____

_____

_____

_____

9) What is the significance of Jesus' response when His family comes looking for Him?

_____

_____

_____

Truth for Today

When people have a great opportunity to hear God's Word and even to see it miraculously demonstrated and then reject it, their guilt is intensified immeasurably. It is far better to have heard nothing of Christ than to hear the truth about Him and yet reject Him. "For if we sin willfully after we have received the knowledge of the truth, there no longer remains a sacrifice for sins, but a certain fearful expectation of judgment" (Heb. 10:26–27 NKJV). The greater the privilege, the greater the responsibility; and the greater the light, the greater the punishment for not receiving it.

Reflecting on the Text

10) Why do you think certain "religious" people are sometimes skeptical about God? Where are you when it comes to doubting Christ?

_____

_____

_____

_____

_____

11) Is your faith overly dependent on experiences? Do you clamor for miraculous manifestations to support your Christian walk? What is the problem with this approach?

_____

_____

_____

_____

12) What steps will you take today to guard against family ties that hinder God's will for you?

_____

_____

_____

_____

13) Jesus said that doing the will of the Father is evidence of being a member of His family. What does doing God's will look like in your life today?

_____

_____

_____

_____

Personal Response

Write out additional reflections, questions you may have, or a prayer.

_____

_____

_____

_____

_____

_____

_____

_____

_____

_____

_____

_____

_____

_____

_____

_____

_____

_____

_____

_____

_____

_____

7

THE KINGDOM PARABLES
Matthew 13:1–58

DRAWING NEAR

Jesus was a master teacher, and nothing showed this better than His use of parables. Think of a time when a story really touched your heart or taught you something. Why are stories useful and powerful tools?

_____

_____

_____

_____

If you had to explain what the kingdom of God is to a six-year-old, what would you say?

_____

_____

_____

_____

THE CONTEXT

Jesus came to earth to offer salvation and the kingdom of God to Israel. But it was clear that the Jewish religious leaders of Jesus' day were rejecting His offer. Did this mean that God's plan was frustrated? And what was to be the nature of the kingdom now? Jesus addresses some of these questions about the kingdom of God with a series of eight parables. The underlying truth of these parables was that the kingdom in its final fulfillment would be postponed until the time that Israel *would* believe in and receive her King. Christ's external, visible kingdom was postponed, but the internal, spiritual kingdom of His saints was established. The Lord reigns in their hearts. Through their lives and testimony He now expresses His will on earth.

Matthew 13 provides us with some foundational truths for understanding the mission of the church. The Lord of the church reveals the nature of the church, as well as the spiritual characteristics of the period of time often referred to as the "church age"—the era between His first and second comings.

Keys to the Text

Parable: The Greek word translated "parable" is a compound word made up of a form of the verb *ballo* ("to throw, lay, or place") and the prefix *para* (meaning "alongside of"). The idea is that of placing or laying something alongside something else for the purpose of comparison. A spiritual or moral truth would often be expressed by laying it alongside, so to speak, a physical example that could be more easily understood. A common, observable object or practice was laid alongside that which was not known or understood, in order to explain it. The known elucidated the unknown. The parable was a common form of Jewish teaching.

Unleashing the Text

Read 13:1–58, noting the key words and definitions next to the passage.

Matthew 13:1–58 (NKJV)

1 On the same day Jesus went out of the house and sat by the sea.

2 And great multitudes were gathered together to Him, so that He got into a boat and sat; and the whole multitude stood on the shore.

wayside (v. 3)—The fields were bordered by paths beaten hard by foot traffic and baking sun.

3 Then He spoke many things to them in parables, saying: "Behold, a sower went out to sow.

4 And as he sowed, some seed fell by the wayside; and the birds came and devoured them.

stony places (v. 5)—very shallow soil that appears fertile but that lies atop a layer of bedrock

5 Some fell on stony places, where they did not have much earth; and they immediately sprang up because they had no depth of earth.

6 But when the sun was up they were scorched, and because they had no root they withered away.

7 And some fell among thorns, and the thorns sprang up and choked them.

8 But others fell on good ground and yielded a crop: some a hundredfold, some sixty, some thirty.

9 He who has ears to hear, let him hear!"

10 And the disciples came and said to Him, "Why do You speak to them in parables?"

it has been given to you (v. 11)—the ability to comprehend spiritual truth is a gracious gift of God, sovereignly bestowed on the elect

the mysteries of the kingdom of heaven (v. 11)—truths which have been hidden from all ages in the past and revealed in the New Testament

11 He answered and said to them, "Because it has been given to you to know the mysteries of the kingdom of heaven, but to them it has not been given.

12 *For whoever has, to him more will be given, and he will have abundance; but whoever does not have, even what he has will be taken away from him.*

13 *Therefore I speak to them in parables, because seeing they do not see, and hearing they do not hear, nor do they understand.*

because seeing they do not see (v. 13)—Their own unbelief is the cause of their spiritual blindness.

14 *And in them the prophecy of Isaiah is fulfilled, which says: 'Hearing you will hear and shall not understand, and seeing you will see and not perceive;*

15 *For the hearts of this people have grown dull. Their ears are hard of hearing, and their eyes they have closed, lest they should see with their eyes and hear with their ears, lest they should understand with their hearts and turn, so that I should heal them.'*

16 *But blessed are your eyes for they see, and your ears for they hear;*

17 *for assuredly, I say to you that many prophets and righteous men desired to see what you see, and did not see it, and to hear what you hear, and did not hear it.*

18 *"Therefore hear the parable of the sower:*

19 *When anyone hears the word of the kingdom, and does not understand it, then the wicked one comes and snatches away what was sown in his heart. This is he who received seed by the wayside.*

wicked one (v. 19)—Because Satan snatches it away, the gospel never penetrates these souls, so it disappears from the surface of their understanding.

20 *But he who received the seed on stony places, this is he who hears the word and immediately receives it with joy;*

stony places (v. 20)—representative of those who make an emotional, superficial commitment to salvation in Christ

21 *yet he has no root in himself, but endures only for a while. For when tribulation or persecution arises because of the word, immediately he stumbles.*

22 *Now he who received seed among the thorns is he who hears the word, and the cares of this world and the deceitfulness of riches choke the word, and he becomes unfruitful.*

who received seed among the thorns (v. 22)—These can't break with the love of money and the world.

23 *But he who received seed on the good ground is he who hears the word and understands it, who indeed bears fruit and produces: some a hundredfold, some sixty, some thirty."*

tares (v. 25)—probably darnel, a type of weed that can hardly be distinguished from wheat until the head matures; a picture of Satan's efforts to devastate the church by mingling his children with God's, in some cases making it impossible for believers to discern true believers from false ones

a tree, so that the birds of the air come and nest in its branches (v. 32)—Palestinian mustard plants are large shrubs, sometimes up to fifteen feet high.

The kingdom of heaven is like leaven (v. 33)—The kingdom is pictured as yeast, multiplying quietly and permeating all that it contacts.

without a parable He did not speak to them (v. 34)—For the rest of His Galilean ministry, all Jesus' public teaching consisted only of parables.

24 *Another parable He put forth to them, saying: "The kingdom of heaven is like a man who sowed good seed in his field;*

25 *but while men slept, his enemy came and sowed tares among the wheat and went his way.*

26 *But when the grain had sprouted and produced a crop, then the tares also appeared.*

27 *So the servants of the owner came and said to him, 'Sir, did you not sow good seed in your field? How then does it have tares?'*

28 *He said to them, 'An enemy has done this.' The servants said to him, 'Do you want us then to go and gather them up?'*

29 *But he said, 'No, lest while you gather up the tares you also uproot the wheat with them.*

30 *Let both grow together until the harvest, and at the time of harvest I will say to the reapers, "First gather together the tares and bind them in bundles to burn them, but gather the wheat into my barn." ' "*

31 *Another parable He put forth to them, saying: "The kingdom of heaven is like a mustard seed, which a man took and sowed in his field,*

32 *which indeed is the least of all the seeds; but when it is grown it is greater than the herbs and becomes a tree, so that the birds of the air come and nest in its branches."*

33 *Another parable He spoke to them: "The kingdom of heaven is like leaven, which a woman took and hid in three measures of meal till it was all leavened."*

34 *All these things Jesus spoke to the multitude in parables; and without a parable He did not speak to them,*

35 *that it might be fulfilled which was spoken by the prophet, saying: "I will open My mouth in parables; I will utter things kept secret from the foundation of the world."*

36 *Then Jesus sent the multitude away and went into the house. And His disciples came to Him, saying, "Explain to us the parable of the tares of the field."*

37 *He answered and said to them: "He who sows the good seed is the Son of Man.*

38 *The field is the world, the good seeds are the sons of the kingdom, but the tares are the sons of the wicked one.*

39 *The enemy who sowed them is the devil, the harvest is the end of the age, and the reapers are the angels.*

40 *Therefore as the tares are gathered and burned in the fire, so it will be at the end of this age.*

41 *The Son of Man will send out His angels, and they will gather out of His kingdom all things that offend, and those who practice lawlessness,*

42 *and will cast them into the furnace of fire. There will be wailing and gnashing of teeth.*

43 *Then the righteous will shine forth as the sun in the kingdom of their Father. He who has ears to hear, let him hear!*

44 *"Again, the kingdom of heaven is like treasure hidden in a field, which a man found and hid; and for joy over it he goes and sells all that he has and buys that field.*

45 *"Again, the kingdom of heaven is like a merchant seeking beautiful pearls,*

46 *who, when he had found one pearl of great price, went and sold all that he had and bought it.*

47 *"Again, the kingdom of heaven is like a dragnet that was cast into the sea and gathered some of every kind,*

48 *which, when it was full, they drew to shore; and they sat down and gathered the good into vessels, but threw the bad away.*

49 *So it will be at the end of the age. The angels will come forth, separate the wicked from among the just,*

50 *and cast them into the furnace of fire. There will be wailing and gnashing of teeth."*

51 *Jesus said to them, "Have you understood all these things?" They said to Him, "Yes, Lord."*

52 *Then He said to them, "Therefore every scribe instructed concerning the kingdom of heaven is like a householder who brings out of his treasure things new and old."*

dragnet (v. 47)—This was a large weighted net dragged along the bottom of the lake, which captured an assortment of marine life, good and bad.

angels (v. 49)—They serve God in judgment (see v. 41 and 2 Thess. 1:7–10).

brings out of his treasure things new and old (v. 52)—The disciples were not to spurn the old for the sake of the new. Rather, the new insights they gleaned from Jesus' parables were to be understood in light of the old truths, and vice versa.

His own country (v. 54)—i.e., Nazareth

His brothers (v. 55)—The fact that Joseph does not actually appear in any of these accounts suggests that he was no longer living.

A prophet . . . in his own country (v. 57)—This is an ancient proverb paralleling the modern saying "Familiarity breeds contempt." They knew Jesus too well as a boy and a young man from their own town—and they concluded that He was nothing special. Verse 58 gives the sad result (see Mark 6:4).

53 *Now it came to pass, when Jesus had finished these parables, that He departed from there.*

54 *And when He had come to His own country, He taught them in their synagogue, so that they were astonished and said, "Where did this Man get this wisdom and these mighty works?*

55 *Is this not the carpenter's son? Is not His mother called Mary? And His brothers James, Joses, Simon, and Judas?*

56 *And His sisters, are they not all with us? Where then did this Man get all these things?"*

57 *So they were offended at Him. But Jesus said to them, "A prophet is not without honor except in his own country and in his own house."*

58 *Now He did not do many mighty works there because of their unbelief.*

1) What exactly is a parable?

_____

_____

_____

2) Who was Jesus' main audience for these parables? How did these stories relate to their lives?

_____

_____

_____

3) What are the lessons contained in the parable of the soils?

_____

_____

_____

4) What was Jesus' explanation to the disciples of the parable of the tares?

_____

_____

_____

5) What is "leaven," and why would Jesus compare the kingdom of heaven to it?

_____

_____

_____

6) What happened when Jesus returned to his hometown of Nazareth (vv. 54–58)?

_____

_____

_____

GOING DEEPER

In telling these parables, Jesus quoted from Isaiah 6:1–10. Read that chapter.

1   *In the year that King Uzziah died, I saw the LORD sitting on a throne, high and lifted up, and the train of His robe filled the temple.*

2   *Above it stood seraphim; each one had six wings: with two he covered his face, with two he covered his feet, and with two he flew.*

3   *And one cried to another and said: "Holy, holy, holy is the LORD of hosts; the whole earth is full of His glory!"*

4   *And the posts of the door were shaken by the voice of him who cried out, and the house was filled with smoke.*

5   *So I said: "Woe is me, for I am undone! Because I am a man of unclean lips, and I dwell in the midst of a people of unclean lips; for my eyes have seen the King, The LORD of hosts."*

6   *Then one of the seraphim flew to me, having in his hand a live coal which he had taken with the tongs from the altar.*

7   *And he touched my mouth with it, and said: "Behold, this has touched your lips; your iniquity is taken away, and your sin purged."*

8   *Also I heard the voice of the LORD, saying: "Whom shall I send, and who will go for Us?" Then I said, "Here am I! Send me."*

9 And He said, "Go, and tell this people: 'Keep on hearing, but do not understand; keep on seeing, but do not perceive.'

10 "Make the heart of this people dull, and their ears heavy, and shut their eyes; lest they see with their eyes, and hear with their ears, and understand with their heart, and return and be healed."

EXPLORING THE MEANING

7) What does this passage in Isaiah tell you about the nature of God and the heart of man?

_____

_____

_____

_____

8) Think about the parable of the soils. What are some "thorns" that threaten to choke out your faith?

_____

_____

_____

_____

9) Jesus compares the kingdom to "treasure," to a "pearl of great price." If this is true (and, of course it is!) how can your life reflect this reality?

_____

_____

_____

_____

10) After having read and pondered these parables, what conclusions can you draw about the kingdom of heaven?

_____

_____

_____

_____

TRUTH FOR TODAY

The ultimate mark of the genuine believer is fruit bearing. The believer not only hears and understands but also indeed bears fruit. Spiritual fruit is the inevitable product of spiritual life. There is spiritual fruit of *attitude* as described by Paul in Galatians: "love, joy, peace, longsuffering, kindness, goodness, faithfulness, gentleness, self-control" (5:22–23 NKJV). The genuine believer also bears fruit of *behavior*, which Paul refers to as "the fruits of righteousness which are by Jesus Christ, to the glory and praise of God" (Phil. 1:11 NKJV). Fruit is the evidence of the Spirit's work in the lives of His children. Jesus declared that true and false branches—those who are genuinely related to Him and those who only seem to be—are distinguished by their bearing or not bearing fruit (John 15:2–5). We are not saved *by* bearing fruit or by any other good work, because we cannot bear spiritual fruit or do any truly good work until after we are saved. But we are saved *for* fruit bearing.

REFLECTING ON THE TEXT

11) How does Jesus' veiling of the truth from unbelievers (by speaking in hard-to-understand parables) fit in with the idea of God's mercy?

_____

_____

_____

_____

_____

12) In light of all we have in the gospel and all the treasures of eternity, why do so many believers act "ho-hum" about Christ and the Christian life?

_____

_____

_____

_____

_____

13) How can you demonstrate gratitude to God this week for opening your eyes to the marvelous truth of the gospel?

_____

_____

_____

_____

_____

_____

PERSONAL RESPONSE

Write out additional reflections, questions you may have, or a prayer.

_____

_____

_____

_____

_____

_____

_____

_____

_____

_____

_____

_____

_____

_____

_____

_____

8

KINGDOMS IN CONFLICT
Matthew 14:1–17:27

DRAWING NEAR

What positive signs or events in the world today give you reason to be optimistic about the days ahead?

_____

_____

_____

_____

What negative or ominous signs tell you that the world is getting worse, and perhaps even moving toward a climactic end?

_____

_____

_____

_____

THE CONTEXT

Our Lord's prophetic parables underscore the truth that some people will believe the gospel, but many people will not. Matthew records in this section a number of incidents in Jesus' life that confirm this spiritual law: the hostility in His hometown of Nazareth, the hard-hearted Herod, the superficial reception of the masses, the worship of the twelve disciples, the desperate faith of a Canaanite woman, and the Jewish leaders who sought to trap Christ. Yet, in the midst of this kingdom conflict, we see the true heart of Jesus for people as He performs more amazing miracles.

Jesus gathers His disciples and gives them a "final exam" of sorts, asking the ultimate question, "Who do you say that I am?" Then, up on a mountaintop experience, God the Father reveals Jesus' glory. Jesus wraps up with some sobering words about what it will involve to live for Him until He returns. Only those who tenaciously believe in Him and steadfastly follow Him will make a difference in a godless world. As you study this lengthy passage, keep the big picture in mind. Though evil is strong, Jesus is Lord.

KEYS TO THE TEXT

Compassion: The Greek verb translated "compassion" means literally "to be moved in one's bowels," where the ancient cultures considered the emotions and feelings to reside. Christ represented the compassionate heart of God. He was never remote or coldly calculating and analytical concerning men's needs but was deeply moved by the suffering, confusion, despair, and spiritual lostness of those around Him. Jesus felt pain, experiencing genuine anguish for the suffering of others, whether they were believer or unbeliever, Jew or Gentile, man or woman, young or old, wealthy or poor. In His great mercy, Christ extended His compassion even to shallow, self-centered thrill seekers. He revealed the loving heart of God toward even those who would not understand or believe and whom He knew would ultimately reject Him.

Jewish Religious Leaders: This group was made up of Pharisees, Sadducees, scribes, and teachers of the law. The *Pharisees* were a small legalistic sect of the Jews known for their rigid adherence to the ceremonial fine points of the Law. Jesus rebuked them for using human tradition to nullify Scripture and for rank hypocrisy. *Scribes* were primarily Pharisees and authorities on Jewish law. Sometimes they are referred to as "lawyers." The *Sadducees* denied the resurrection of the dead and the existence of angels, and accepted only the Pentateuch as authoritative. In the days of Herod, their sect controlled the temple.

UNLEASHING THE TEXT

Read 14:1–17:27, noting the key words and definitions next to the passage.

Matthew 14:1–17:27 (NKJV)

1 At that time Herod the tetrarch heard the report about Jesus

2 and said to his servants, "This is John the Baptist; he is risen from the dead, and therefore these powers are at work in him."

Herodias, his brother Philip's wife (14:3)—John was outraged that a ruler in Israel would commit such a sin as incest openly, so he rebuked Herod severely (v. 4) and was promptly imprisoned and later killed (Mark 6:14–29).

3 For Herod had laid hold of John and bound him, and put him in prison for the sake of Herodias, his brother Philip's wife.

4 Because John had said to him, "It is not lawful for you to have her."

5 And although he wanted to put him to death, he feared the multitude, because they counted him as a prophet.

6 But when Herod's birthday was celebrated, the

daughter of Herodias danced before them and pleased Herod.

7 *Therefore he promised with an oath to give her whatever she might ask.*

8 *So she, having been prompted by her mother, said, "Give me John the Baptist's head here on a platter."*

9 *And the king was sorry; nevertheless, because of the oaths and because of those who sat with him, he commanded it to be given to her.*

because of the oaths (v. 9)— Herod was widely known for his duplicity, so it was not honesty that he was concerned about, but rather the appearance of things.

10 *So he sent and had John beheaded in prison.*

11 *And his head was brought on a platter and given to the girl, and she brought it to her mother.*

12 *Then his disciples came and took away the body and buried it, and went and told Jesus.*

13 *When Jesus heard it, He departed from there by boat to a deserted place by Himself. But when the multitudes heard it, they followed Him on foot from the cities.*

14 *And when Jesus went out He saw a great multitude; and He was moved with compassion for them, and healed their sick.*

15 *When it was evening, His disciples came to Him, saying, "This is a deserted place, and the hour is already late. Send the multitudes away, that they may go into the villages and buy themselves food."*

16 *But Jesus said to them, "They do not need to go away. You give them something to eat."*

give them something to eat (v. 16)—Jesus knew they did not have enough food to feed the crowd. He wanted the disciples to state it plainly so the record would be clear that a miracle by His power occurred.

17 *And they said to Him, "We have here only five loaves and two fish."*

18 *He said, "Bring them here to Me."*

19 *Then He commanded the multitudes to sit down on the grass. And He took the five loaves and the two fish, and looking up to heaven, He blessed and broke and gave the loaves to the disciples; and the disciples gave to the multitudes.*

20 *So they all ate and were filled, and they took up twelve baskets full of the fragments that remained.*

21 *Now those who had eaten were about five thousand men, besides women and children.*

fourth watch (v. 25)—3:00–6:00 AM

Gennesaret (v. 34)—a town on the northwest shore of the Sea of Galilee

22 *Immediately Jesus made His disciples get into the boat and go before Him to the other side, while He sent the multitudes away.*

23 *And when He had sent the multitudes away, He went up on the mountain by Himself to pray. Now when evening came, He was alone there.*

24 *But the boat was now in the middle of the sea, tossed by the waves, for the wind was contrary.*

25 *Now in the fourth watch of the night Jesus went to them, walking on the sea.*

26 *And when the disciples saw Him walking on the sea, they were troubled, saying, "It is a ghost!" And they cried out for fear.*

27 *But immediately Jesus spoke to them, saying, "Be of good cheer! It is I; do not be afraid."*

28 *And Peter answered Him and said, "Lord, if it is You, command me to come to You on the water."*

29 *So He said, "Come." And when Peter had come down out of the boat, he walked on the water to go to Jesus.*

30 *But when he saw that the wind was boisterous, he was afraid; and beginning to sink he cried out, saying, "Lord, save me!"*

31 *And immediately Jesus stretched out His hand and caught him, and said to him, "O you of little faith, why did you doubt?"*

32 *And when they got into the boat, the wind ceased.*

33 *Then those who were in the boat came and worshiped Him, saying, "Truly You are the Son of God."*

34 *When they had crossed over, they came to the land of Gennesaret.*

35 *And when the men of that place recognized Him, they sent out into all that surrounding region, brought to Him all who were sick,*

36 *and begged Him that they might only touch the hem of His garment. And as many as touched it were made perfectly well.*

15:1 *Then the scribes and Pharisees who were from Jerusalem came to Jesus, saying,*

2 *"Why do Your disciples transgress the tradition of the elders? For they do not wash their hands when they eat bread."*

3 *He answered and said to them, "Why do you also transgress the commandment of God because of your tradition?*

4 *For God commanded, saying, 'Honor your father and your mother'; and, 'He who curses father or mother, let him be put to death.'*

5 *But you say, 'Whoever says to his father or mother, "Whatever profit you might have received from me is a gift to God"—*

6 *then he need not honor his father or mother.' Thus you have made the commandment of God of no effect by your tradition.*

7 *Hypocrites! Well did Isaiah prophesy about you, saying:*

8 *'These people draw near to Me with their mouth, And honor Me with their lips, But their heart is far from Me.*

9 *And in vain they worship Me, Teaching as doctrines the commandments of men.' "*

10 *When He had called the multitude to Himself, He said to them, "Hear and understand:*

11 *Not what goes into the mouth defiles a man; but what comes out of the mouth, this defiles a man."*

12 *Then His disciples came and said to Him, "Do You know that the Pharisees were offended when they heard this saying?"*

13 *But He answered and said, "Every plant which My heavenly Father has not planted will be uprooted.*

14 *Let them alone. They are blind leaders of the blind. And if the blind leads the blind, both will fall into a ditch."*

15 *Then Peter answered and said to Him, "Explain this parable to us."*

16 *So Jesus said, "Are you also still without understanding?*

17 *Do you not yet understand that whatever enters the mouth goes into the stomach and is eliminated?*

tradition of the elders (15:2)—This was not the God-given, so-called Mosaic law but the extrabiblical law that had existed only in oral form and only since the time of the Babylonian captivity.

transgress (v. 3)—Some people deviously claimed they could not financially assist their parents because they had dedicated a certain sum of money to God, who was greater than their parents.

what comes out of the mouth, this defiles a man (v. 11)—People might defile themselves ceremonially (under the Old Covenant) by eating something unclean, but they would defile themselves morally by saying something sinful.

this parable (v. 15)—This parable is not at all hard to understand, but it was hard for even the disciples to accept; years later, Peter still found it hard to accept that all foods are clean (Acts 10:14).

the little dogs (v. 26)—Christ employed a word here that speaks of a family pet. His words with this woman are not to be understood as harsh or unfeeling. In fact, He was tenderly drawing from her an expression of her faith.

18 *But those things which proceed out of the mouth come from the heart, and they defile a man.*

19 *For out of the heart proceed evil thoughts, murders, adulteries, fornications, thefts, false witness, blasphemies.*

20 *These are the things which defile a man, but to eat with unwashed hands does not defile a man."*

21 *Then Jesus went out from there and departed to the region of Tyre and Sidon.*

22 *And behold, a woman of Canaan came from that region and cried out to Him, saying, "Have mercy on me, O Lord, Son of David! My daughter is severely demon-possessed."*

23 *But He answered her not a word. And His disciples came and urged Him, saying, "Send her away, for she cries out after us."*

24 *But He answered and said, "I was not sent except to the lost sheep of the house of Israel."*

25 *Then she came and worshiped Him, saying, "Lord, help me!"*

26 *But He answered and said, "It is not good to take the children's bread and throw it to the little dogs."*

27 *And she said, "Yes, Lord, yet even the little dogs eat the crumbs which fall from their masters' table."*

28 *Then Jesus answered and said to her, "O woman, great is your faith! Let it be to you as you desire." And her daughter was healed from that very hour.*

29 *Jesus departed from there, skirted the Sea of Galilee, and went up on the mountain and sat down there.*

30 *Then great multitudes came to Him, having with them the lame, blind, mute, maimed, and many others; and they laid them down at Jesus' feet, and He healed them.*

31 *So the multitude marveled when they saw the mute speaking, the maimed made whole, the lame walking, and the blind seeing; and they glorified the God of Israel.*

32 *Now Jesus called His disciples to Himself and said, "I have compassion on the multitude, because they*

have now continued with Me three days and have nothing to eat. And I do not want to send them away hungry, lest they faint on the way."

33 *Then His disciples said to Him, "Where could we get enough bread in the wilderness to fill such a great multitude?"*

34 *Jesus said to them, "How many loaves do you have?" And they said, "Seven, and a few little fish."*

35 *So He commanded the multitude to sit down on the ground.*

36 *And He took the seven loaves and the fish and gave thanks, broke them and gave them to His disciples; and the disciples gave to the multitude.*

37 *So they all ate and were filled, and they took up seven large baskets full of the fragments that were left.*

38 *Now those who ate were four thousand men, besides women and children.*

39 *And He sent away the multitude, got into the boat, and came to the region of Magdala.*

16:1 *Then the Pharisees and Sadducees came, and testing Him asked that He would show them a sign from heaven.*

2 *He answered and said to them, "When it is evening you say, 'It will be fair weather, for the sky is red';*

3 *and in the morning, 'It will be foul weather today, for the sky is red and threatening.' Hypocrites! You know how to discern the face of the sky, but you cannot discern the signs of the times.*

4 *A wicked and adulterous generation seeks after a sign, and no sign shall be given to it except the sign of the prophet Jonah." And He left them and departed.*

5 *Now when His disciples had come to the other side, they had forgotten to take bread.*

6 *Then Jesus said to them, "Take heed and beware of the leaven of the Pharisees and the Sadducees."*

7 *And they reasoned among themselves, saying, "It is because we have taken no bread."*

Where could we get enough bread (v. 33)—No wonder our Lord often called them men of little faith, when they asked a question like this in the light of the recent feeding of the five thousand (see 14:13–21).

the leaven of the Pharisees and the Sadducees (16:6)—i.e., their dangerous influence

the living God (v. 16)—an Old Testament name for Jehovah, as contrasted with dead, dumb idols

flesh and blood has not revealed *this* **to you** (v. 17)—God the Father had opened Peter's eyes to the full significance of those claims and revealed to him who Jesus really was; this confession of Peter's personal faith was made possible by a divinely regenerated heart.

You are Peter (*Petros*)**, and on this rock** (*petra*) (v. 18)—This was a simple play on words. The boulderlike truth of Christ's identity, *petra*, came from the mouth of one who was called a small stone, *Petros*.

the gates of Hades (v. 18)—a Jewish phrase referring to death, since Hades is the place of punishment for the spirits of dead unbelievers

the keys of the kingdom of heaven (v. 19)—representative of authority, given here to Peter (and by extension to all other believers)

bind . . . loose (v. 19)—Any duly constituted body of believers, acting in accord with God's Word, has the authority to declare the judgment of heaven based on the principles of the Word.

8 But Jesus, being aware of it, said to them, "O you of little faith, why do you reason among yourselves because you have brought no bread?

9 Do you not yet understand, or remember the five loaves of the five thousand and how many baskets you took up?

10 Nor the seven loaves of the four thousand and how many large baskets you took up?

11 How is it you do not understand that I did not speak to you concerning bread?—but to beware of the leaven of the Pharisees and Sadducees."

12 Then they understood that He did not tell them to beware of the leaven of bread, but of the doctrine of the Pharisees and Sadducees.

13 When Jesus came into the region of Caesarea Philippi, He asked His disciples, saying, "Who do men say that I, the Son of Man, am?"

14 So they said, "Some say John the Baptist, some Elijah, and others Jeremiah or one of the prophets."

15 He said to them, "But who do you say that I am?"

16 Simon Peter answered and said, "You are the Christ, the Son of the living God."

17 Jesus answered and said to him, "Blessed are you, Simon Bar-Jonah, for flesh and blood has not revealed this to you, but My Father who is in heaven.

18 And I also say to you that you are Peter, and on this rock I will build My church, and the gates of Hades shall not prevail against it.

19 And I will give you the keys of the kingdom of heaven, and whatever you bind on earth will be bound in heaven, and whatever you loose on earth will be loosed in heaven."

20 Then He commanded His disciples that they should tell no one that He was Jesus the Christ.

21 From that time Jesus began to show to His disciples that He must go to Jerusalem, and suffer many things from the elders and chief priests and scribes, and be killed, and be raised the third day.

22 *Then Peter took Him aside and began to rebuke Him, saying, "Far be it from You, Lord; this shall not happen to You!"*

23 *But He turned and said to Peter, "Get behind Me, Satan! You are an offense to Me, for you are not mindful of the things of God, but the things of men."*

Get behind Me, Satan! (v. 23)—Jesus suggested that Peter was being a mouthpiece for Satan, who was trying to prevent any kind of divine atonement for sin.

24 *Then Jesus said to His disciples, "If anyone desires to come after Me, let him deny himself, and take up his cross, and follow Me.*

25 *For whoever desires to save his life will lose it, but whoever loses his life for My sake will find it.*

26 *For what profit is it to a man if he gains the whole world, and loses his own soul? Or what will a man give in exchange for his soul?*

27 *For the Son of Man will come in the glory of His Father with His angels, and then He will reward each according to his works.*

28 *Assuredly, I say to you, there are some standing here who shall not taste death till they see the Son of Man coming in His kingdom."*

some standing (v. 28)—Since the word for "kingdom" can be translated "royal splendor," it seems most natural to interpret this as a reference to the Transfiguration, which Peter, James, and John, would witness six days later.

17:1 *Now after six days Jesus took Peter, James, and John his brother, led them up on a high mountain by themselves;*

2 *and He was transfigured before them. His face shone like the sun, and His clothes became as white as the light.*

3 *And behold, Moses and Elijah appeared to them, talking with Him.*

Moses and Elijah (17:3)—representing the Law and the Prophets respectively

4 *Then Peter answered and said to Jesus, "Lord, it is good for us to be here; if You wish, let us make here three tabernacles: one for You, one for Moses, and one for Elijah."*

three tabernacles (v. 4)—Undoubtedly a reference to the booths used to celebrate the Feast of Tabernacles. Peter was expressing a wish to stay in that place.

5 *While he was still speaking, behold, a bright cloud overshadowed them; and suddenly a voice came out of the cloud, saying, "This is My beloved Son, in whom I am well pleased. Hear Him!"*

6 *And when the disciples heard it, they fell on their faces and were greatly afraid.*

7 *But Jesus came and touched them and said, "Arise, and do not be afraid."*

Elijah has come already (v. 12)—John came in the spirit and power of Elijah, and the Jewish leaders had killed him.

8 *When they had lifted up their eyes, they saw no one but Jesus only.*

9 *Now as they came down from the mountain, Jesus commanded them, saying, "Tell the vision to no one until the Son of Man is risen from the dead."*

10 *And His disciples asked Him, saying, "Why then do the scribes say that Elijah must come first?"*

11 *Jesus answered and said to them, "Indeed, Elijah is coming first and will restore all things.*

12 *But I say to you that Elijah has come already, and they did not know him but did to him whatever they wished. Likewise the Son of Man is also about to suffer at their hands."*

13 *Then the disciples understood that He spoke to them of John the Baptist.*

14 *And when they had come to the multitude, a man came to Him, kneeling down to Him and saying,*

15 *"Lord, have mercy on my son, for he is an epileptic and suffers severely; for he often falls into the fire and often into the water.*

16 *So I brought him to Your disciples, but they could not cure him."*

17 *Then Jesus answered and said, "O faithless and perverse generation, how long shall I be with you? How long shall I bear with you? Bring him here to Me."*

18 *And Jesus rebuked the demon, and it came out of him; and the child was cured from that very hour.*

19 *Then the disciples came to Jesus privately and said, "Why could we not cast it out?"*

faith as a mustard seed (v. 20)—The object of all genuine faith—even the weak, mustard-seed variety—is God.

20 *So Jesus said to them, "Because of your unbelief; for assuredly, I say to you, if you have faith as a mustard seed, you will say to this mountain, 'Move from here to there,' and it will move; and nothing will be impossible for you.*

21 *However, this kind does not go out except by prayer and fasting."*

22 *Now while they were staying in Galilee, Jesus said to them, "The Son of Man is about to be betrayed into the hands of men,*

23 *and they will kill Him, and the third day He will be*
   raised up." And they were exceedingly sorrowful.
24 *When they had come to Capernaum, those who*
   received the temple tax came to Peter and said,
   "Does your Teacher not pay the temple tax?"
25 *He said, "Yes." And when he had come into the*
   house, Jesus anticipated him, saying, "What do
   you think, Simon? From whom do the kings of the
   earth take customs or taxes, from their sons or from
   strangers?"
26 *Peter said to Him, "From strangers." Jesus said to*
   him, "Then the sons are free.
27 *Nevertheless, lest we offend them, go to the sea, cast*
   in a hook, and take the fish that comes up first. And
   when you have opened its mouth, you will find a
   piece of money; take that and give it to them for Me
   and you."

the temple tax (v. 24)—This half-shekel tax was collected annually from every male over twenty for the upkeep of the temple. Jesus, as God's Son, was exempt from the tax, but to avoid offense, He paid on behalf of Himself and Peter.

1) Why did King Herod deal with John the Baptist so severely? What was Jesus' response (14:1–13)?

_____

_____

_____

_____

_____

2) The account of the feeding of the five thousand is the only miracle, other than the resurrection, that is recorded in all four Gospels. What are the significant details of this work of Christ?

_____

_____

_____

_____

3) Jesus took the Pharisees to task for what violations of the Mosaic law (15:1–20)?

_____

_____

_____

_____

4) What happened when Jesus quizzed His disciples as to His "reputation" (16:13–20)? What was the significance of this moment?

_____

_____

_____

_____

5) Skim the passage and identify the various encounters Jesus had with different individuals. What do you learn about Jesus from these encounters?

_____

_____

_____

_____

6) What affirmation did God the Father give to Jesus' ministry (17:1–5)?

_____

_____

_____

_____

GOING DEEPER

Read Mark 7:1–16 to see Jesus clashing with the Pharisees again.

1   *Then the Pharisees and some of the scribes came together to Him, having come from Jerusalem.*
2   *Now when they saw some of His disciples eat bread with defiled, that is, with unwashed hands, they found fault.*

3   For the Pharisees and all the Jews do not eat unless they wash their hands
     in a special way, holding the tradition of the elders.
4   When they come from the marketplace, they do not eat unless they wash.
     And there are many other things which they have received and hold, like
     the washing of cups, pitchers, copper vessels, and couches.
5   Then the Pharisees and scribes asked Him, "Why do Your disciples not
     walk according to the tradition of the elders, but eat bread with unwashed
     hands?"
6   He answered and said to them, "Well did Isaiah prophesy of you
     hypocrites, as it is written: 'This people honors Me with their lips, but their
     heart is far from Me.
7   And in vain they worship Me, teaching as doctrines the commandments of
     men.'
8   For laying aside the commandment of God, you hold the tradition of
     men— the washing of pitchers and cups, and many other such things you
     do."
9   He said to them, "All too well you reject the commandment of God, that
     you may keep your tradition.
10 For Moses said, 'Honor your father and your mother'; and, 'He who curses
     father or mother, let him be put to death.'
11 But you say, 'If a man says to his father or mother, "Whatever profit you
     might have received from me is Corban"—' (that is, a gift to God),
12 then you no longer let him do anything for his father or his mother,
13 making the word of God of no effect through your tradition which you
     have handed down. And many such things you do."
14 When He had called all the multitude to Himself, He said to them, "Hear
     Me, everyone, and understand:
15 There is nothing that enters a man from outside which can defile him; but
     the things which come out of him, those are the things that defile a man.
16 If anyone has ears to hear, let him hear!"

EXPLORING THE MEANING

7) How did Jesus respond to those who valued man-made religious
tradition over divine truth?

_____

_____

_____

8) Why did Jesus rebuff the Pharisees and Sadducees when they asked Him for a sign from heaven (Matt. 16:1–4)?

_____

_____

_____

_____

9) What is significant about the way Jesus describes His church (16:18)?

_____

_____

_____

_____

10) What did the Transfiguration reveal? Why do you think the disciples who witnessed this event were not forever altered by it?

_____

_____

_____

_____

11) The temple tax incident—what lessons should we draw from this surprising turn of events?

_____

_____

_____

_____

Truth for Today

Those who heard and saw Jesus did not reject Him for *lack* of evidence, but *in spite of* overwhelming evidence. They did not reject Him because they lacked the truth, but because they rejected the truth. They refused forgiveness because they wanted to keep their sins. They denied the light because they preferred darkness. The reason for rejecting the Lord has always been that men prefer their own way to His.

REFLECTING ON THE TEXT

12) Again (Matt. 16:24–26), Christ calls His followers to unflinching and radical devotion. Read the words again. What impact do they have on your heart and will?

_____

_____

_____

_____

_____

13) Thinking specifically about the Transfiguration, what can you do today to give Christ the glory He deserves?

_____

_____

_____

_____

_____

14) This lesson has covered more than four chapters of Matthew's gospel, and a number of amazing events. What stands out to you most? What passage do you want to go back and explore further? Why?

_____

_____

_____

_____

_____

PERSONAL RESPONSE

Write out additional reflections, questions you may have, or a prayer.

_____

_____

_____

_____

_____

_____

_____

_____

_____

_____

_____

_____

_____

_____

_____

_____

_____

_____

_____

_____

_____

_____

_____

_____

_____

9

CHILDREN OF THE KINGDOM
Matthew 18:1–35

DRAWING NEAR

Jesus loved and welcomed children wherever he went. What are some of your favorite childhood memories?

_____

_____

_____

What do you miss most about the carefree days of childhood?

_____

_____

_____

THE CONTEXT

Scripture describes and identifies the people of God by many names. But more frequently than anything else we are called *children*—children of promise, children of the day, children of the light, beloved children, dear children, and children of God. As believers we can rejoice in the wonderful truth that, through Christ, we have become God's own children, adopted through grace. Consequently, we bear the image of God's family and are joint heirs with Jesus Christ of everything God possesses. We enjoy God's love, care, protection, power, and other resources in abundance for all eternity.

But there is another side to our being children. In Scripture believers are also referred to as children in the sense that we are incomplete, weak, dependent, undeveloped, unskilled, vulnerable, and immature. Matthew 18 focuses on these immature, unperfected, childlike qualities that believers demonstrate as they mutually develop into conformity to the fullness of the stature of Jesus Christ.

This chapter is a single sermon by our Lord on the specific theme of the childlikeness of the believer, speaking directly to the reality that we are spiritual children with all the weaknesses that childhood implies. The first lesson in this masterful sermon is that everyone who enters the kingdom does so as a child. Jesus then teaches that all of us in the kingdom must be treated as children, cared for as children, disciplined as children, and forgiven as children. It is no exaggeration to say that this is the single greatest discourse our Lord ever gave on life among the redeemed people in His church. We shall attempt to recover these truths that are so vital, powerful, and needed by the church in every age and place.

Keys to the Text

Like a Child: The Greek word *paidion*, translated "little child" (18:2), identifies a very young child, sometimes even an infant. This particular child was perhaps a toddler, just old enough to run to Jesus when He called him. Because the disciples, arguing over who was the greatest, were likely in Peter's house, the child may have belonged to Peter's family and already been well-known to Jesus. In any case, he readily responded and allowed himself to be taken up into Jesus' arms (Mark 9:36). Jesus loved children, and they loved Him, and as He sat before the disciples, holding this small child in His arms, He had a beautiful setting in which to teach them profound lessons about the childlikeness of believers.

Unleashing the Text

Read 18:1–35, noting the key words and definitions next to the passage.

Matthew 18:1–35 (NKJV)

1 *At that time the disciples came to Jesus, saying, "Who then is greatest in the kingdom of heaven?"*

2 *Then Jesus called a little child to Him, set him in the midst of them,*

become as little children (v. 3)—a picture of conversion; i.e., faith being the simple, helpless, trusting dependence of those who have no resources, achievements, or accomplishments to commend themselves with toward God

3 *and said, "Assuredly, I say to you, unless you are converted and become as little children, you will by no means enter the kingdom of heaven.*

4 *Therefore whoever humbles himself as this little child is the greatest in the kingdom of heaven.*

5 *Whoever receives one little child like this in My name receives Me.*

millstone (v. 6)—a large stone used for grinding grain; literally, "the millstone of an ass"—a stone so large it took a donkey to turn it. Gentiles used this form of execution, and therefore it was particularly repulsive to the Jews.

6 *"Whoever causes one of these little ones who believe in Me to sin, it would be better for him if a millstone were hung around his neck, and he were drowned in the depth of the sea.*

7 *Woe to the world because of offenses! For offenses must come, but woe to that man by whom the offense comes!*

8 *"If your hand or foot causes you to sin, cut it off and*

cast it from you. It is better for you to enter into life lame or maimed, rather than having two hands or two feet, to be cast into the everlasting fire.

9 And if your eye causes you to sin, pluck it out and cast it from you. It is better for you to enter into life with one eye, rather than having two eyes, to be cast into hell fire.

10 "Take heed that you do not despise one of these little ones, for I say to you that in heaven their angels always see the face of My Father who is in heaven.

11 For the Son of Man has come to save that which was lost.

12 "What do you think? If a man has a hundred sheep, and one of them goes astray, does he not leave the ninety-nine and go to the mountains to seek the one that is straying?

13 And if he should find it, assuredly, I say to you, he rejoices more over that sheep than over the ninety-nine that did not go astray.

14 Even so it is not the will of your Father who is in heaven that one of these little ones should perish.

15 "Moreover if your brother sins against you, go and tell him his fault between you and him alone. If he hears you, you have gained your brother.

16 But if he will not hear, take with you one or two more, that 'by the mouth of two or three witnesses every word may be established.'

17 And if he refuses to hear them, tell it to the church. But if he refuses even to hear the church, let him be to you like a heathen and a tax collector.

18 "Assuredly, I say to you, whatever you bind on earth will be bound in heaven, and whatever you loose on earth will be loosed in heaven.

do not despise (v. 10)—i.e., spurn or belittle another believer by treating him or her unkindly or indifferently

their angels (v. 10)—This is not, as commonly believed, a statement about personal guardian angels. Rather, the pronoun is collective and indicates that believers are served by angels in general. These angels are pictured "always" watching the face of God so as to hear His command to them to help a believer when needed. It is extremely serious to treat any fellow believer with contempt since God and the holy angels are so concerned for their well-being.

perish (v. 14)—Here, the word is a reference to spiritual devastation rather than utter eternal destruction. God's children can never perish in the ultimate sense (see John 10:28).

if your brother sins against you (v. 15)—This prescription for church discipline in verses 15–17 must be read in light of the parable of the lost sheep in verses. 12–14. The goal of this process is restoration. Step one is to "tell him his fault" privately.

if he will not hear (v. 16)—I.e., if he/she remains impenitent, follow step two: "take with you one or two more," to fulfill the principle of Deuteronomy 19:15.

tell it to the church (v. 17)—The third step of church discipline requires that the matter involving the unrepentant Christian be reported to the whole assembly (v. 17)—so that all may lovingly pursue the sinning brother's reconciliation.

But failing that, step four means that the offender must be excommunicated, regarded by the church as "a heathen and a tax collector" (5:46). The idea is not merely to punish the offender, or to shun him completely, but to remove him as a detrimental influence from the fellowship of the church, and henceforth to regard him as an evangelistic prospect rather than as a brother. Ultimately, the sin for which he is excommunicated is a hard-hearted impenitence.

if two of you agree on earth (v. 19)—This promise applies to the issue of discipline discussed in verses 15–17; the "two of you" spoken of here refers back to the two or three witnesses involved in step two of the discipline process.

two or three (v. 20)—Though Jewish tradition requires at least ten men (a *minyan*) to constitute a synagogue or even hold public prayer, here Christ promised to be present in the midst of an even smaller flock—"two or three witnesses" gathered in His name for the purpose of discipline.

Up to seven times (v. 21)—Peter thought he was being magnanimous, since Israel's leading rabbis, citing several verses from Amos (1:3, 6, 9, 11, 13), taught that since God forgave Israel's enemies only three times, it was presumptuous and unnecessary to forgive anyone more than three times.

seventy times seven (v. 22)—innumerable times

ten thousand talents (v. 24)—Representative of an incomprehensible amount of money, the talent was the largest denomination of currency, and "ten thousand" in common parlance signified an infinite number.

forgave him (v. 27)—picturing the generous, compassionate forgiveness of God to a pleading sinner who owes him an unpayable debt (see Col. 2:14)

a hundred denarii (v. 28)—about three months' wages; not a negligible amount by normal standards, but a pittance in comparison to what the servant had been forgiven

19 *"Again I say to you that if two of you agree on earth concerning anything that they ask, it will be done for them by My Father in heaven.*

20 *For where two or three are gathered together in My name, I am there in the midst of them."*

21 *Then Peter came to Him and said, "Lord, how often shall my brother sin against me, and I forgive him? Up to seven times?"*

22 *Jesus said to him, "I do not say to you, up to seven times, but up to seventy times seven.*

23 *Therefore the kingdom of heaven is like a certain king who wanted to settle accounts with his servants.*

24 *And when he had begun to settle accounts, one was brought to him who owed him ten thousand talents.*

25 *But as he was not able to pay, his master commanded that he be sold, with his wife and children and all that he had, and that payment be made.*

26 *The servant therefore fell down before him, saying, 'Master, have patience with me, and I will pay you all.'*

27 *Then the master of that servant was moved with compassion, released him, and forgave him the debt.*

28 *"But that servant went out and found one of his fellow servants who owed him a hundred denarii; and he laid hands on him and took him by the throat, saying, 'Pay me what you owe!'*

29 *So his fellow servant fell down at his feet and begged him, saying, 'Have patience with me, and I will pay you all.'*

30 *And he would not, but went and threw him into prison till he should pay the debt.*

31 *So when his fellow servants saw what had been done, they were very grieved, and came and told their master all that had been done.*

32 *Then his master, after he had called him, said to him, 'You wicked servant! I forgave you all that debt because you begged me.*

33 *Should you not also have had compassion on your fellow servant, just as I had pity on you?'*

34 *And his master was angry, and delivered him to the torturers until he should pay all that was due to him.*

35 *"So My heavenly Father also will do to you if each of you, from his heart, does not forgive his brother his trespasses."*

his master was angry (v. 34)—Because He is holy and just, God is always angry at sin, including the sins of His children (see Heb. 12:5–11).

torturers (v. 34)—not executioners, but those administering severe discipline

1) How did Jesus teach His bickering disciples a lesson by hugging a small child?

_____

_____

_____

2) What does Jesus say about a believer who leads others into sin, directly or indirectly?

_____

_____

_____

3) Matthew 18:15–19 speaks about church discipline. What does Jesus call believers to do when a brother is in sin?

_____

_____

_____

4) What was Jesus' response to Peter's question about forgiveness?

_____

_____

_____

Going Deeper

There is another version of the parable of the lost sheep in Luke 15. Read that entire chapter and see what it reveals about the heart of God.

1   *Then all the tax collectors and the sinners drew near to Him to hear Him.*
2   *And the Pharisees and scribes complained, saying, "This Man receives sinners and eats with them."*
3   *So He spoke this parable to them, saying:*
4   *"What man of you, having a hundred sheep, if he loses one of them, does not leave the ninety-nine in the wilderness, and go after the one which is lost until he finds it?*
5   *And when he has found it, he lays it on his shoulders, rejoicing.*
6   *And when he comes home, he calls together his friends and neighbors, saying to them, 'Rejoice with me, for I have found my sheep which was lost!'*
7   *I say to you that likewise there will be more joy in heaven over one sinner who repents than over ninety-nine just persons who need no repentance.*
8   *"Or what woman, having ten silver coins, if she loses one coin, does not light a lamp, sweep the house, and search carefully until she finds it?*
9   *And when she has found it, she calls her friends and neighbors together, saying, 'Rejoice with me, for I have found the piece which I lost!'*
10 *Likewise, I say to you, there is joy in the presence of the angels of God over one sinner who repents."*
11 *Then He said: "A certain man had two sons.*
12 *And the younger of them said to his father, 'Father, give me the portion of goods that falls to me.' So he divided to them his livelihood.*
13 *And not many days after, the younger son gathered all together, journeyed to a far country, and there wasted his possessions with prodigal living.*
14 *But when he had spent all, there arose a severe famine in that land, and he began to be in want.*
15 *Then he went and joined himself to a citizen of that country, and he sent him into his fields to feed swine.*
16 *And he would gladly have filled his stomach with the pods that the swine ate, and no one gave him anything.*
17 *"But when he came to himself, he said, 'How many of my father's hired servants have bread enough and to spare, and I perish with hunger!*
18 *I will arise and go to my father, and will say to him, "Father, I have sinned against heaven and before you,*
19 *and I am no longer worthy to be called your son. Make me like one of your hired servants."'*

20 *"And he arose and came to his father. But when he was still a great way off, his father saw him and had compassion, and ran and fell on his neck and kissed him.*

21 *And the son said to him, 'Father, I have sinned against heaven and in your sight, and am no longer worthy to be called your son.'*

22 *"But the father said to his servants, 'Bring out the best robe and put it on him, and put a ring on his hand and sandals on his feet.*

23 *And bring the fatted calf here and kill it, and let us eat and be merry;*

24 *for this my son was dead and is alive again; he was lost and is found.' And they began to be merry.*

25 *"Now his older son was in the field. And as he came and drew near to the house, he heard music and dancing.*

26 *So he called one of the servants and asked what these things meant.*

27 *And he said to him, 'Your brother has come, and because he has received him safe and sound, your father has killed the fatted calf.'*

28 *"But he was angry and would not go in. Therefore his father came out and pleaded with him.*

29 *So he answered and said to his father, 'Lo, these many years I have been serving you; I never transgressed your commandment at any time; and yet you never gave me a young goat, that I might make merry with my friends.*

30 *But as soon as this son of yours came, who has devoured your livelihood with harlots, you killed the fatted calf for him.'*

31 *"And he said to him, 'Son, you are always with me, and all that I have is yours.*

32 *It was right that we should make merry and be glad, for your brother was dead and is alive again, and was lost and is found.' "*

EXPLORING THE MEANING

5) Why are the consequences so severe for those who lead others astray?

_____

_____

_____

_____

_____

6) Have you ever been part of a church that practiced church discipline? What happened? What is the "upside" of church discipline? What are the potential "risks"?

_____

_____

_____

_____

7) How does it alter your view of God to see Him compared by Matthew to a caring shepherd who searches frantically for one lost individual?

_____

_____

_____

_____

8) Why is the forgiveness advocated by Christ so rare? Why is it so hard to forgive?

_____

_____

_____

_____

_____

TRUTH FOR TODAY

To be converted requires people to become like children, Jesus explained. A little child is simple, dependent, helpless, unaffected, unpretentious, unambitious. Children are not sinless or naturally unselfish, and they display their fallen nature from the earliest age. But they are nevertheless naive and unassuming, trusting of others and without ambition for grandeur and greatness.

It is the person who humbles himself as this child, Jesus declared, who is greatest in the kingdom of heaven (see 18:4). The verb behind "humbles" is *tapeinoō*, which has the literal meaning of "making low." In God's eyes, the one who lowers himself is the one who is elevated; the one who genuinely considers himself to be the least is the one God considers to be the greatest. "The greatest among you shall be your servant," Jesus told the self-righteous Pharisees. "And whoever exalts himself shall be humbled; and he who humbles himself will be exalted" (Matt. 23:11–12 NKJV). The person who is not willing to humble himself as Jesus "humbled Himself" (Phil. 2:8) will have no place in Jesus' kingdom. For self-righteous Jews who exalted themselves so highly as to think God was pleased with them for their own goodness, this was a shattering blow.

REFLECTING ON THE TEXT

9) This entire chapter is, in effect, Jesus' response to a petty argument. It is Christ's insistence that His followers demonstrate humility. Now that you have spent some time studying this trait, how would you explain it or describe it?

_____

_____

_____

_____

10) The next time someone says or does something against you that seems unforgivable, offer a prayer like this:

O God, put in me the heart of forgiveness, so that I may commune with You in the fullness of fellowship and joy and not experience the chastening that comes when You don't forgive me because I won't forgive a brother or sister in Christ. May I remember that for everyone who sins against me I have many, many more times sinned against You. Yet You have always forgiven me. At no time has any of my sin caused me to forfeit my eternal life; therefore, no one else's sin should cause them to forfeit my love and my mercy toward them.

Or write your own prayer that expresses the truth of Matthew 18:21–25.

_____

_____

_____

_____

_____

11) What do you sense God prompting you to do today to humble yourself, to become more like a little child?

_____

_____

_____

_____

_____

_____

Personal Response

Write out additional reflections, questions you may have, or a prayer.

_____

_____

_____

_____

_____

_____

_____

_____

_____

_____

_____

_____

10

ROYAL PRONOUNCEMENTS
Matthew 19:1–23:39

DRAWING NEAR

When you think of Jesus, do you think of Him as a king? Why or why not?

_____

_____

_____

What does it mean to you that Jesus is indeed the King of kings?

_____

_____

_____

THE CONTEXT

In this section of Matthew's gospel we see Christ as the King of heaven, who is rejected by His own people. Jesus is moving relentlessly toward the hour of His suffering and death. The hostility of the Jewish leaders is growing. Every event and conversation in these tense, final days affords the Lord one more opportunity to shine the light of God's truth into the world's darkness. He contrasts legalistic religion with the grace and truth of God, the values of earth with the realities of heaven. He speaks bluntly about a number of vitally important subjects— marriage and divorce, eternal life, true greatness, and eternal judgment. He also performs provocative acts such as purging the sellers in the temple and cursing a fruitless fig tree. Through all of this, we see Jesus' great love and compassion.

This is a lengthy passage, and we will not be able to study it in depth. As you read through, notice the main points of Jesus' teaching.

KEYS TO THE TEXT

Christ Is King: In ancient times the coronation of a monarch involved the display of great splendor and pageantry. The king would be dressed in the most expensive robes and jewels and would be driven through his capital city in an ornate carriage drawn by stately horses. Accompanying him would be his courtiers and foreign dignitaries, and following that would be a large retinue of the nation's finest soldiers. At the climax of the events, the king would be presented with a scepter or would participate in some other ritual signifying the transfer of power and authority into his hands. Every part of the ceremony was designed to highlight the majesty, glory, power, and dignity of the king. Jesus' entry into Jerusalem on a donkey (Matt. 21:1–11) portrays the most significant coronation the world has yet seen, but it was a coronation in marked contrast to the usual kind. Jesus was affirmed as King and was, in a sense, inaugurated into His kingship. But there was no pomp, no splendor, and only a brief sort of pageantry.

UNLEASHING THE TEXT

Read 19:1–23:39, noting the key words and definitions next to the passage.

Matthew 19:1–23:39 (NKJV)

1 *Now it came to pass, when Jesus had finished these sayings, that He departed from Galilee and came to the region of Judea beyond the Jordan.*

2 *And great multitudes followed Him, and He healed them there.*

3 *The Pharisees also came to Him, testing Him, and saying to Him, "Is it lawful for a man to divorce his wife for just any reason?"*

4 *And He answered and said to them, "Have you not read that He who made them at the beginning 'made them male and female,'*

5 *and said, 'For this reason a man shall leave his father and mother and be joined to his wife, and the two shall become one flesh'?*

6 *So then, they are no longer two but one flesh. Therefore what God has joined together, let not man separate."*

7 *They said to Him, "Why then did Moses command to give a certificate of divorce, and to put her away?"*

8 *He said to them, "Moses, because of the hardness of your hearts, permitted you to divorce your wives, but from the beginning it was not so.*

9 *And I say to you, whoever divorces his wife, except for sexual immorality, and marries another, commits adultery; and whoever marries her who is divorced commits adultery."*

Is it lawful (v. 3)—A hotly debated difference of opinion existed between the Rabbis Shammai and Hillel (both near-contemporaries of Christ). The Shammaites interpreted the Law rigidly and permitted a man to divorce his wife only if she was guilty of sexual immorality; the Hillelites took a wholly pragmatic approach and permitted a man to divorce his wife indiscriminately.

Why then did Moses command to give a certificate of divorce (v. 7)—The Pharisees misrepresented Deuteronomy 24:1-4 as a "command" for divorce, when it was really a limitation on remarriage in the event of a divorce.

because of the hardness of your hearts (v. 8)—Divorce is only to be a last-resort response to hard-hearted sexual immorality (v. 9).

sexual immorality (v. 9)—a term that encompasses all sorts of sexual sins

10 *His disciples said to Him, "If such is the case of the man with his wife, it is better not to marry."*

11 *But He said to them, "All cannot accept this saying, but only those to whom it has been given:*

12 *For there are eunuchs who were born thus from their mother's womb, and there are eunuchs who were made eunuchs by men, and there are eunuchs who have made themselves eunuchs for the kingdom of heaven's sake. He who is able to accept it, let him accept it."*

13 *Then little children were brought to Him that He might put His hands on them and pray, but the disciples rebuked them.*

14 *But Jesus said, "Let the little children come to Me, and do not forbid them; for of such is the kingdom of heaven."*

15 *And He laid His hands on them and departed from there.*

16 *Now behold, one came and said to Him, "Good Teacher, what good thing shall I do that I may have eternal life?"*

17 *So He said to him, "Why do you call Me good? No one is good but One, that is, God. But if you want to enter into life, keep the commandments."*

18 *He said to Him, "Which ones?" Jesus said, " 'You shall not murder,' 'You shall not commit adultery,' 'You shall not steal,' 'You shall not bear false witness,'*

19 *'Honor your father and your mother,' and, 'You shall love your neighbor as yourself.' "*

20 *The young man said to Him, "All these things I have kept from my youth. What do I still lack?"*

21 *Jesus said to him, "If you want to be perfect, go, sell what you have and give to the poor, and you will have treasure in heaven; and come, follow Me."*

22 *But when the young man heard that saying, he went away sorrowful, for he had great possessions.*

23 *Then Jesus said to His disciples, "Assuredly, I say to you that it is hard for a rich man to enter the kingdom of heaven.*

it is better not to marry (v. 10)—The disciples correctly understood the binding nature of marriage and that Jesus was setting a very high standard.

of such (v. 14)—God shows a special mercy to those who, because of age or mental deficiency, are incapable of either faith or willful unbelief.

if you want to enter into life, keep the commandments (v. 17)—Jesus wanted to impress on the young man the absolute futility of seeking salvation by his own merit.

I have kept (v. 20)—The self-righteous young man would not admit to sin.

go, sell what you have and give to the poor (v. 21)—Jesus was exposing the young man's true heart. He was guilty of loving himself and his possessions more than his neighbors, and he was unwilling to surrender all at Christ's bidding.

camel . . . eye of a needle (v. 24)—I.e., it is impossible.

24 *And again I say to you, it is easier for a camel to go through the eye of a needle than for a rich man to enter the kingdom of God."*

25 *When His disciples heard it, they were greatly astonished, saying, "Who then can be saved?"*

26 *But Jesus looked at them and said to them, "With men this is impossible, but with God all things are possible."*

27 *Then Peter answered and said to Him, "See, we have left all and followed You. Therefore what shall we have?"*

28 *So Jesus said to them, "Assuredly I say to you, that in the regeneration, when the Son of Man sits on the throne of His glory, you who have followed Me will also sit on twelve thrones, judging the twelve tribes of Israel.*

29 *And everyone who has left houses or brothers or sisters or father or mother or wife or children or lands, for My name's sake, shall receive a hundredfold, and inherit eternal life.*

30 *But many who are first will be last, and the last first.*

hire laborers (20:1)—Day laborers stood in the marketplace place from dawn, hoping to be hired for the harvest work. The workday began at 6:00 AM and went to 6:00 PM.

20:1 *"For the kingdom of heaven is like a landowner who went out early in the morning to hire laborers for his vineyard.*

2 *Now when he had agreed with the laborers for a denarius a day, he sent them into his vineyard.*

3 *And he went out about the third hour and saw others standing idle in the marketplace,*

4 *and said to them, 'You also go into the vineyard, and whatever is right I will give you.' So they went.*

5 *Again he went out about the sixth and the ninth hour, and did likewise.*

6 *And about the eleventh hour he went out and found others standing idle, and said to them, 'Why have you been standing here idle all day?'*

7 *They said to him, 'Because no one hired us.' He said to them, 'You also go into the vineyard, and whatever is right you will receive.'*

8 *"So when evening had come, the owner of the*

vineyard said to his steward, 'Call the laborers and give them their wages, beginning with the last to the first.'

9 And when those came who were hired about the eleventh hour, they each received a denarius.

10 But when the first came, they supposed that they would receive more; and they likewise received each a denarius.

11 And when they had received it, they complained against the landowner,

12 saying, 'These last men have worked only one hour, and you made them equal to us who have borne the burden and the heat of the day.'

13 But he answered one of them and said, 'Friend, I am doing you no wrong. Did you not agree with me for a denarius?

14 Take what is yours and go your way. I wish to give to this last man the same as to you.

15 Is it not lawful for me to do what I wish with my own things? Or is your eye evil because I am good?'

16 So the last will be first, and the first last. For many are called, but few chosen."

17 Now Jesus, going up to Jerusalem, took the twelve disciples aside on the road and said to them,

18 "Behold, we are going up to Jerusalem, and the Son of Man will be betrayed to the chief priests and to the scribes; and they will condemn Him to death,

19 and deliver Him to the Gentiles to mock and to scourge and to crucify. And the third day He will rise again."

20 Then the mother of Zebedee's sons came to Him with her sons, kneeling down and asking something from Him.

21 And He said to her, "What do you wish?" She said to Him, "Grant that these two sons of mine may sit, one on Your right hand and the other on the left, in Your kingdom."

22 But Jesus answered and said, "You do not know what you ask. Are you able to drink the cup that I am about to drink, and be baptized with the

I am doing you no wrong (v. 13)—Everyone received a full day's wage, to their shock (vv. 9–11); it was his privilege to extend the same generosity to all (v. 15; see Rom. 9:15).

the last will be first, and the first last (v. 16)—Everyone finishes in a dead heat.

Grant . . . these two sons of mine (v. 21)—James and John had enlisted their mother to convey their proud, self-seeking request to Jesus.

the cup that I am about to drink (v. 22)—the cup of God's wrath

baptism that I am baptized with?" They said to Him, "We are able."

23 So He said to them, "You will indeed drink My cup, and be baptized with the baptism that I am baptized with; but to sit on My right hand and on My left is not Mine to give, but it is for those for whom it is prepared by My Father."

24 And when the ten heard it, they were greatly displeased with the two brothers.

25 But Jesus called them to Himself and said, "You know that the rulers of the Gentiles lord it over them, and those who are great exercise authority over them.

26 Yet it shall not be so among you; but whoever desires to become great among you, let him be your servant.

27 And whoever desires to be first among you, let him be your slave—

28 just as the Son of Man did not come to be served, but to serve, and to give His life a ransom for many."

to give His life a ransom for many (v. 28)—The word translated "for" means "in the place of," underscoring the substitutionary nature of Christ's sacrifice; a "ransom" is a price paid to redeem a slave or a prisoner.

29 Now as they went out of Jericho, a great multitude followed Him.

30 And behold, two blind men sitting by the road, when they heard that Jesus was passing by, cried out, saying, "Have mercy on us, O Lord, Son of David!"

31 Then the multitude warned them that they should be quiet; but they cried out all the more, saying, "Have mercy on us, O Lord, Son of David!"

32 So Jesus stood still and called them, and said, "What do you want Me to do for you?"

33 They said to Him, "Lord, that our eyes may be opened."

34 So Jesus had compassion and touched their eyes. And immediately their eyes received sight, and they followed Him.

21:1 Now when they drew near Jerusalem, and came to Bethphage, at the Mount of Olives, then Jesus sent two disciples,

2 *saying to them, "Go into the village opposite you,*
   and immediately you will find a donkey tied, and a
   colt with her. Loose them and bring them to Me.

3 *And if anyone says anything to you, you shall say,*
   'The Lord has need of them,' and immediately he
   will send them."

4 *All this was done that it might be fulfilled which was*
   spoken by the prophet, saying:

5 *"Tell the daughter of Zion, 'Behold, your King is*
   coming to you, Lowly, and sitting on a donkey, A
   colt, the foal of a donkey.' "

A colt, the foal of a donkey (21:5)—an exact quotation from Zechariah 9:9 (see Isa. 62:11)

6 *So the disciples went and did as Jesus commanded*
   them.

7 *They brought the donkey and the colt, laid their*
   clothes on them, and set Him on them.

8 *And a very great multitude spread their clothes on*
   the road; others cut down branches from the trees
   and spread them on the road.

9 *Then the multitudes who went before and those who*
   followed cried out, saying: "Hosanna to the Son of
   David! 'Blessed is He who comes in the name of the
   LORD!' Hosanna in the highest!"

Hosanna (v. 9)—transliterates the Hebrew expression which is translated "Save now" in Psalm 118:25

10 *And when He had come into Jerusalem, all the city*
   was moved, saying, "Who is this?"

11 *So the multitudes said, "This is Jesus, the prophet*
   from Nazareth of Galilee."

12 *Then Jesus went into the temple of God and drove*
   out all those who bought and sold in the temple,
   and overturned the tables of the money changers
   and the seats of those who sold doves.

drove out (v. 12)—This was the second time Jesus had cleansed the temple. John 2:14–16 describes a similar incident at the beginning of Christ's public ministry.

13 *And He said to them, "It is written, 'My house shall*
   be called a house of prayer,' but you have made it a
   'den of thieves.' "

14 *Then the blind and the lame came to Him in the*
   temple, and He healed them.

15 *But when the chief priests and scribes saw the*
   wonderful things that He did, and the children
   crying out in the temple and saying, "Hosanna to
   the Son of David!" they were indignant

The baptism of John—where was it from? (v. 25)—Jesus asked a question that placed the religious leaders in an impossible dilemma because John was widely revered by the people. They could not affirm John's ministry without condemning themselves. And if they denied John's legitimacy, they feared the response of the people (v. 26).

16 and said to Him, "Do You hear what these are saying?" And Jesus said to them, "Yes. Have you never read, 'Out of the mouth of babes and nursing infants You have perfected praise'?"

17 Then He left them and went out of the city to Bethany, and He lodged there.

18 Now in the morning, as He returned to the city, He was hungry.

19 And seeing a fig tree by the road, He came to it and found nothing on it but leaves, and said to it, "Let no fruit grow on you ever again." Immediately the fig tree withered away.

20 And when the disciples saw it, they marveled, saying, "How did the fig tree wither away so soon?"

21 So Jesus answered and said to them, "Assuredly, I say to you, if you have faith and do not doubt, you will not only do what was done to the fig tree, but also if you say to this mountain, 'Be removed and be cast into the sea,' it will be done.

22 And whatever things you ask in prayer, believing, you will receive."

23 Now when He came into the temple, the chief priests and the elders of the people confronted Him as He was teaching, and said, "By what authority are You doing these things? And who gave You this authority?"

24 But Jesus answered and said to them, "I also will ask you one thing, which if you tell Me, I likewise will tell you by what authority I do these things:

25 The baptism of John—where was it from? From heaven or from men?" And they reasoned among themselves, saying, "If we say, 'From heaven,' He will say to us, 'Why then did you not believe him?'

26 But if we say, 'From men,' we fear the multitude, for all count John as a prophet."

27 So they answered Jesus and said, "We do not know." And He said to them, "Neither will I tell you by what authority I do these things.

28 "But what do you think? A man had two sons, and he came to the first and said, 'Son, go, work today in my vineyard.'

29 He answered and said, 'I will not,' but afterward he regretted it and went.

30 Then he came to the second and said likewise. And he answered and said, 'I go, sir,' but he did not go.

31 Which of the two did the will of his father?" They said to Him, "The first." Jesus said to them, "Assuredly, I say to you that tax collectors and harlots enter the kingdom of God before you.

32 For John came to you in the way of righteousness, and you did not believe him; but tax collectors and harlots believed him; and when you saw it, you did not afterward relent and believe him.

33 "Hear another parable: There was a certain landowner who planted a vineyard and set a hedge around it, dug a winepress in it and built a tower. And he leased it to vinedressers and went into a far country.

34 Now when vintage-time drew near, he sent his servants to the vinedressers, that they might receive its fruit.

35 And the vinedressers took his servants, beat one, killed one, and stoned another.

36 Again he sent other servants, more than the first, and they did likewise to them.

37 Then last of all he sent his son to them, saying, 'They will respect my son.'

38 But when the vinedressers saw the son, they said among themselves, 'This is the heir. Come, let us kill him and seize his inheritance.'

39 So they took him and cast him out of the vineyard and killed him.

40 "Therefore, when the owner of the vineyard comes, what will he do to those vinedressers?"

41 They said to Him, "He will destroy those wicked men miserably, and lease his vineyard to other vinedressers who will render to him the fruits in their seasons."

my son (v. 37)—This person represents the Lord Jesus Christ, whom they killed (vv. 38–39) and thereby incurred divine judgment (v. 41).

this stone (v. 44)—Christ is "a stone of stumbling and a rock of offense" to unbelievers (Isa. 8:14; 1 Pet. 2:8).

burned up their city (22:7)— The judgment Jesus described anticipated the destruction of Jerusalem in AD 70.

42 Jesus said to them, "Have you never read in the Scriptures: 'The stone which the builders rejected Has become the chief cornerstone. This was the LORD's doing, And it is marvelous in our eyes' ?

43 "Therefore I say to you, the kingdom of God will be taken from you and given to a nation bearing the fruits of it.

44 And whoever falls on this stone will be broken; but on whomever it falls, it will grind him to powder."

45 Now when the chief priests and Pharisees heard His parables, they perceived that He was speaking of them.

46 But when they sought to lay hands on Him, they feared the multitudes, because they took Him for a prophet.

22:1 And Jesus answered and spoke to them again by parables and said:

2 "The kingdom of heaven is like a certain king who arranged a marriage for his son,

3 and sent out his servants to call those who were invited to the wedding; and they were not willing to come.

4 Again, he sent out other servants, saying, 'Tell those who are invited, "See, I have prepared my dinner; my oxen and fatted cattle are killed, and all things are ready. Come to the wedding." '

5 But they made light of it and went their ways, one to his own farm, another to his business.

6 And the rest seized his servants, treated them spitefully, and killed them.

7 But when the king heard about it, he was furious. And he sent out his armies, destroyed those murderers, and burned up their city.

8 Then he said to his servants, 'The wedding is ready, but those who were invited were not worthy.

9 Therefore go into the highways, and as many as you find, invite to the wedding.'

10 So those servants went out into the highways and gathered together all whom they found, both bad

and good. And the wedding hall was filled with guests.

11 "But when the king came in to see the guests, he saw a man there who did not have on a wedding garment.

12 So he said to him, 'Friend, how did you come in here without a wedding garment?' And he was speechless.

13 Then the king said to the servants, 'Bind him hand and foot, take him away, and cast him into outer darkness; there will be weeping and gnashing of teeth.'

14 "For many are called, but few are chosen."

15 Then the Pharisees went and plotted how they might entangle Him in His talk.

16 And they sent to Him their disciples with the Herodians, saying, "Teacher, we know that You are true, and teach the way of God in truth; nor do You care about anyone, for You do not regard the person of men.

17 Tell us, therefore, what do You think? Is it lawful to pay taxes to Caesar, or not?"

18 But Jesus perceived their wickedness, and said, "Why do you test Me, you hypocrites?

19 Show Me the tax money." So they brought Him a denarius.

20 And He said to them, "Whose image and inscription is this?"

21 They said to Him, "Caesar's." And He said to them, "Render therefore to Caesar the things that are Caesar's, and to God the things that are God's."

22 When they had heard these words, they marveled, and left Him and went their way.

23 The same day the Sadducees, who say there is no resurrection, came to Him and asked Him,

24 saying: "Teacher, Moses said that if a man dies, having no children, his brother shall marry his wife and raise up offspring for his brother.

25 Now there were with us seven brothers. The first died after he had married, and having no offspring, left his wife to his brother.

a wedding garment (v. 11)—This man's lack of a proper garment indicates he had purposely rejected the king's own gracious provision of the necessary attire.

Is it lawful to pay taxes to Caesar, or not? (v. 17)—At issue was the poll tax, an annual fee that Rome assessed to finance its occupying armies. All Roman taxes were hated by the people; if He answered no, the Herodians would charge Him with treason against Rome; if He said yes, the Pharisees would accuse Him of disloyalty to the Jewish nation.

denarius (v. 19)—a silver coin, the value of a day's wage for a Roman soldier

his brother shall marry his wife (v. 24)—This refers to the law of levirate marriage, found in Deuteronomy 25:5–10, a provision to ensure that family lines were kept intact and widows were cared for.

26 *Likewise the second also, and the third, even to the seventh.*

27 *Last of all the woman died also.*

28 *Therefore, in the resurrection, whose wife of the seven will she be? For they all had her."*

29 *Jesus answered and said to them, "You are mistaken, not knowing the Scriptures nor the power of God.*

30 *For in the resurrection they neither marry nor are given in marriage, but are like angels of God in heaven.*

31 *But concerning the resurrection of the dead, have you not read what was spoken to you by God, saying,*

32 *'I am the God of Abraham, the God of Isaac, and the God of Jacob' ? God is not the God of the dead, but of the living."*

33 *And when the multitudes heard this, they were astonished at His teaching.*

34 *But when the Pharisees heard that He had silenced the Sadducees, they gathered together.*

35 *Then one of them, a lawyer, asked Him a question, testing Him, and saying,*

36 *"Teacher, which is the great commandment in the law?"*

37 *Jesus said to him, "'You shall love the LORD your God with all your heart, with all your soul, and with all your mind.'*

38 *This is the first and great commandment.*

39 *And the second is like it: 'You shall love your neighbor as yourself.'*

40 *On these two commandments hang all the Law and the Prophets."*

41 *While the Pharisees were gathered together, Jesus asked them,*

42 *saying, "What do you think about the Christ? Whose Son is He?" They said to Him, "The Son of David."*

43 *He said to them, "How then does David in the Spirit call Him 'Lord,' saying:*

heart . . . soul . . . mind (v. 37)— The use of the various terms is not meant to delineate distinct human faculties, but to underscore the completeness of the kind of love Jesus called for.

love your neighbor as yourself (v. 39)—not a mandate for self-love, but a call for believers to measure their love for others by what they wish for themselves

44 '*The* L*ORD* *said to my Lord, "Sit at My right hand,*
Till I make Your enemies Your footstool" '?

45 *If David then calls Him 'Lord,' how is He his Son?"*

46 *And no one was able to answer Him a word, nor*
from that day on did anyone dare question Him
anymore.

23:1 *Then Jesus spoke to the multitudes and to His*
disciples,

2 *saying: "The scribes and the Pharisees sit in Moses'*
seat.

3 *Therefore whatever they tell you to observe, that*
observe and do, but do not do according to their
works; for they say, and do not do.

4 *For they bind heavy burdens, hard to bear, and lay*
them on men's shoulders; but they themselves will
not move them with one of their fingers.

5 *But all their works they do to be seen by men. They*
make their phylacteries broad and enlarge the
borders of their garments.

6 *They love the best places at feasts, the best seats in*
the synagogues,

7 *greetings in the marketplaces, and to be called by*
men, 'Rabbi, Rabbi.'

8 *But you, do not be called 'Rabbi'; for One is your*
Teacher, the Christ, and you are all brethren.

9 *Do not call anyone on earth your father; for One is*
your Father, He who is in heaven.

10 *And do not be called teachers; for One is your*
Teacher, the Christ.

11 *But he who is greatest among you shall be your*
servant.

12 *And whoever exalts himself will be humbled, and he*
who humbles himself will be exalted.

13 *"But woe to you, scribes and Pharisees, hypocrites!*
For you shut up the kingdom of heaven against
men; for you neither go in yourselves, nor do you
allow those who are entering to go in.

14 *Woe to you, scribes and Pharisees, hypocrites! For*
you devour widows' houses, and for a pretense

Moses' seat (23:2)—equivalent to a university's "chair of philosophy"; i.e., to have the highest authority to instruct people in the law

phylacteries (v. 5)—These were leather boxes worn by men during prayer, each containing a parchment on which was written passages from Exodus and Deuteronomy.

117

make long prayers. Therefore you will receive greater condemnation.

proselyte (v. 15)—a Gentile convert to Judaism

15 *"Woe to you, scribes and Pharisees, hypocrites! For you travel land and sea to win one proselyte, and when he is won, you make him twice as much a son of hell as yourselves.*

16 *"Woe to you, blind guides, who say, 'Whoever swears by the temple, it is nothing; but whoever swears by the gold of the temple, he is obliged to perform it.'*

17 *Fools and blind! For which is greater, the gold or the temple that sanctifies the gold?*

18 *And, 'Whoever swears by the altar, it is nothing; but whoever swears by the gift that is on it, he is obliged to perform it.'*

19 *Fools and blind! For which is greater, the gift or the altar that sanctifies the gift?*

20 *Therefore he who swears by the altar, swears by it and by all things on it.*

21 *He who swears by the temple, swears by it and by Him who dwells in it.*

22 *And he who swears by heaven, swears by the throne of God and by Him who sits on it.*

tithe of mint and anise and cummin (v. 23)—garden herbs, not really the kind of farm produce that the tithe was designed to cover (Lev. 27:30)

23 *"Woe to you, scribes and Pharisees, hypocrites! For you pay tithe of mint and anise and cummin, and have neglected the weightier matters of the law: justice and mercy and faith. These you ought to have done, without leaving the others undone.*

24 *Blind guides, who strain out a gnat and swallow a camel!*

you cleanse the outside (v. 25)—The Pharisees lived their lives as if external appearance was more important than internal reality. That was the very essence of their hypocrisy, and Jesus rebuked them for it repeatedly.

25 *"Woe to you, scribes and Pharisees, hypocrites! For you cleanse the outside of the cup and dish, but inside they are full of extortion and self-indulgence.*

26 *Blind Pharisee, first cleanse the inside of the cup and dish, that the outside of them may be clean also.*

27 *"Woe to you, scribes and Pharisees, hypocrites! For you are like whitewashed tombs which indeed appear beautiful outwardly, but inside are full of dead men's bones and all uncleanness.*

28 *Even so you also outwardly appear righteous to men, but inside you are full of hypocrisy and lawlessness.*

29 *"Woe to you, scribes and Pharisees, hypocrites! Because you build the tombs of the prophets and adorn the monuments of the righteous,*

30 *and say, 'If we had lived in the days of our fathers, we would not have been partakers with them in the blood of the prophets.'*

31 *"Therefore you are witnesses against yourselves that you are sons of those who murdered the prophets.*

32 *Fill up, then, the measure of your fathers' guilt.*

33 *Serpents, brood of vipers! How can you escape the condemnation of hell?*

34 *Therefore, indeed, I send you prophets, wise men, and scribes: some of them you will kill and crucify, and some of them you will scourge in your synagogues and persecute from city to city,*

35 *that on you may come all the righteous blood shed on the earth, from the blood of righteous Abel to the blood of Zechariah, son of Berechiah, whom you murdered between the temple and the altar.*

36 *Assuredly, I say to you, all these things will come upon this generation.*

37 *"O Jerusalem, Jerusalem, the one who kills the prophets and stones those who are sent to her! How often I wanted to gather your children together, as a hen gathers her chicks under her wings, but you were not willing!*

38 *See! Your house is left to you desolate;*

39 *for I say to you, you shall see Me no more till you say, 'Blessed is He who comes in the name of the LORD!'"*

I wanted . . . but you were not willing! (v. 37)—God sometimes expresses a wish for that which He does not sovereignly bring to pass, revealing His compassionate desire to do good to all.

1) In your own words, summarize Jesus' teaching on divorce.

_____

_____

_____

_____

2) How did Jesus respond to the rich young man (19:16–24)? Why?

_____

_____

_____

_____

3) What is the underlying message of the parable of the laborers (20:1–16)?

_____

_____

_____

_____

_____

4) What main events transpired when Jesus first arrived in Jerusalem (21:1–17)? What do these events signify about who Jesus was?

_____

_____

_____

5) What is the point of the parable of the marriage feast (22:1–14)?

_____

_____

_____

_____

6) Explain the greatest commandment in your own words (22:37–39). How can a person know when he or she is being obedient to this text?

_____

_____

_____

_____

_____

GOING DEEPER

Read Mark 12:1–13 for more insight about Jesus' enemies during this time in Jerusalem.

1   *Then He began to speak to them in parables: "A man planted a vineyard and set a hedge around it, dug a place for the wine vat and built a tower. And he leased it to vinedressers and went into a far country.*

2   *Now at vintage-time he sent a servant to the vinedressers, that he might receive some of the fruit of the vineyard from the vinedressers.*

3   *And they took him and beat him and sent him away empty-handed.*

4   *Again he sent them another servant, and at him they threw stones, wounded him in the head, and sent him away shamefully treated.*

5   *And again he sent another, and him they killed; and many others, beating some and killing some.*

6   *Therefore still having one son, his beloved, he also sent him to them last, saying, 'They will respect my son.'*

7   *But those vinedressers said among themselves, 'This is the heir. Come, let us kill him, and the inheritance will be ours.'*

8   *So they took him and killed him and cast him out of the vineyard.*

9   *"Therefore what will the owner of the vineyard do? He will come and destroy the vinedressers, and give the vineyard to others.*

10 *Have you not even read this Scripture: 'The stone which the builders rejected Has become the chief cornerstone.*

11 *This was the LORD's doing, and it is marvelous in our eyes'?"*

12 *And they sought to lay hands on Him, but feared the multitude, for they knew He had spoken the parable against them. So they left Him and went away.*

13 *Then they sent to Him some of the Pharisees and the Herodians, to catch Him in His words.*

EXPLORING THE MEANING

7) What did Jesus' parable about the vineyard in Mark's passage reveal? Why did the Pharisees want to kill Jesus?

_____

_____

_____

8) How did Jesus characterize the religious leaders in Matthew 23? Which of their traits are still common among some believers today?

_____

_____

_____

9) What does Jesus' lament over Jerusalem suggest about the heart of God (Matt. 23:37–39)? The heart of man?

_____

_____

_____

TRUTH FOR TODAY

Most of the people we read about in Matthew's gospel wanted Jesus on their own terms. They would not bow to a King who was not of their liking, even though He was the Son of God. They wanted Jesus to destroy Rome but not their cherished sins or their hypocritical, superficial religion. But He would not deliver them on their terms, and they would not be delivered on His. He was not a Messiah who came to offer a panacea of external peace in the world but to offer the infinitely greater blessing of internal peace with God.

Many people today are open to a Jesus who they think will give them wealth, health, success, happiness, and the worldly things they want. Like the multitude at the triumphal entry, they will loudly acclaim Jesus as long as they believe He will satisfy their selfish desires. But like the same multitude a few days later, they will reject and denounce Him when He does not deliver as expected. When His Word confronts them with their sin and their need of a Savior, they curse Him and turn away. The words of the multitude were right, but their hearts were not. In any case, He had come at that time not to be crowned but to be crucified. He will be crowned one day in a way that is perfectly befitting.

REFLECTING ON THE TEXT

10) In what specific and practical ways can modern-day Christians treat Jesus as their true King?

_____

_____

_____

_____

_____

11) In this passage, Christ reminds His followers again and again of eternal realities. There is much material to digest here. What incident or statement stands out to you most? Why?

_____

_____

_____

_____

_____

12) What step of obedience will you take today to demonstrate that you love Christ with all your heart, soul, and mind? What act of disobedience will you renounce?

_____

_____

_____

_____

_____

_____

PERSONAL RESPONSE

Write out additional reflections, questions you may have, or a prayer.

11

THE KING TELLS THE FUTURE
Matthew 24:1–25:46

DRAWING NEAR

Many people are fascinated by futuristic movies, horoscopes, psychic predictions, etc. Why do you think this is? What's behind this obsession with the future?

_____

_____

_____

When you think about your eternal future as a believer, what are you looking forward to the most?

_____

_____

_____

THE CONTEXT

Jesus' message in Matthew 24–25 is commonly known as the Olivet discourse, so named because it was delivered to the disciples on the Mount of Olives. The theme of the discourse is Christ's second coming at the end of the present age to establish his millennial kingdom on earth. The message was prompted by the disciples' question, "Tell us, when will these things be? And what will be the sign of Your coming, and of the end of the age?" The answer Jesus gave is the longest answer given to any question asked in the New Testament. The truths here are absolutely essential for understanding Jesus' return and the amazing events associated with it. It is the revelation of our Lord, directly from His own lips, about His return to earth in glory and power.

The teaching of the Olivet discourse is much debated and frequently misunderstood, largely because it is viewed through the lens of a particular theological system or interpretive scheme that makes the message appear complex and enigmatic. But the disciples were not learned men, and Jesus' purpose was to give them clarity and encouragement, not complexity and anxiety. As you read, try to take Jesus' words as simply and straightforwardly as possible.

KEYS TO THE TEXT

Second Coming: This refers to Christ's future return to the earth at the end of the present age. Although the Bible explicitly speaks of Christ's appearance as a "second time," the phrase "second coming" occurs nowhere in the New Testament. Many passages, however, speak of His return. In the New Testament alone it is referred to over three hundred times. The night before His crucifixion, Jesus told His apostles that He would return (Matt. 24:27; John 14:3). When Jesus ascended into heaven, two angels appeared to His followers, saying that He would return in the same manner as they had seen Him go (Acts 1:11). The New Testament is filled with expectancy of His coming, even as Christians should be today. (*Nelson's New Illustrated Bible Dictionary*)

UNLEASHING THE TEXT

Read 24:1–25:46, noting the key words and definitions next to the passage.

the buildings of the temple (24:1)—the temple begun by Herod the Great in 20 BC and still under construction when the Romans destroyed it in AD 70; at the time of Christ, one of the most impressive structures in the world

not one stone shall be left here (v. 2)—These words were literally fulfilled in AD 70. The heat from the fires set by Titus, the Roman general, was so intense that the stones crumbled.

Mount of Olives (v. 3)—directly opposite the temple, across the Kidron Valley to the east

what will be the sign of Your coming (v. 3)—The disciples did not envision a second coming in the far-off future; they were speaking of His coming in triumph as Messiah, an event which they assumed would occur presently.

sorrows (v. 8)—The word means "birth pangs" and refers to famines, earthquakes, and conflicts that will get notably worse at the end of the era as the arrival of Messiah draws near.

Matthew 24:1–25:46 (NKJV)

1 *Then Jesus went out and departed from the temple, and His disciples came up to show Him the buildings of the temple.*

2 *And Jesus said to them, "Do you not see all these things? Assuredly, I say to you, not one stone shall be left here upon another, that shall not be thrown down."*

3 *Now as He sat on the Mount of Olives, the disciples came to Him privately, saying, "Tell us, when will these things be? And what will be the sign of Your coming, and of the end of the age?"*

4 *And Jesus answered and said to them: "Take heed that no one deceives you.*

5 *For many will come in My name, saying, 'I am the Christ,' and will deceive many.*

6 *And you will hear of wars and rumors of wars. See that you are not troubled; for all these things must come to pass, but the end is not yet.*

7 *For nation will rise against nation, and kingdom against kingdom. And there will be famines, pestilences, and earthquakes in various places.*

8 *All these are the beginning of sorrows.*

9 "Then they will deliver you up to tribulation and kill you, and you will be hated by all nations for My name's sake.

10 And then many will be offended, will betray one another, and will hate one another.

11 Then many false prophets will rise up and deceive many.

12 And because lawlessness will abound, the love of many will grow cold.

13 But he who endures to the end shall be saved.

14 And this gospel of the kingdom will be preached in all the world as a witness to all the nations, and then the end will come.

15 "Therefore when you see the 'abomination of desolation,' spoken of by Daniel the prophet, standing in the holy place" (whoever reads, let him understand),

16 "then let those who are in Judea flee to the mountains.

17 Let him who is on the housetop not go down to take anything out of his house.

18 And let him who is in the field not go back to get his clothes.

19 But woe to those who are pregnant and to those who are nursing babies in those days!

20 And pray that your flight may not be in winter or on the Sabbath.

21 For then there will be great tribulation, such as has not been since the beginning of the world until this time, no, nor ever shall be.

22 And unless those days were shortened, no flesh would be saved; but for the elect's sake those days will be shortened.

23 "Then if anyone says to you, 'Look, here is the Christ!' or 'There!' do not believe it.

24 For false christs and false prophets will rise and show great signs and wonders to deceive, if possible, even the elect.

25 See, I have told you beforehand.

endures to the end ... be saved (v. 13)—Scripture everywhere teaches that God, as part of His saving work, secures our perseverance; those who do fall away from Christ give conclusive proof that they were never truly believers to begin with (1 John 2:19).

abomination of desolation (v. 15)—This phrase originally referred to the desecration of the temple by Antiochus Epiphanes, king of Syria, in the second century BC. Antiochus invaded Jerusalem in 168 BC, made the altar into a shrine to Zeus, and even sacrificed pigs on it. However, Jesus clearly was looking toward a future "abomination of desolation" when the Antichrist sets up an image in the temple during the future tribulation.

great tribulation (v. 21)—The words "has not been" and "nor ever shall be"—along with the description that follows—identify this as the yet-future time in which God's wrath shall be poured out upon the earth.

do not believe it (v. 26)—No one should consider the claims of self-styled messiahs, because all of them are false. When Christ returns, no one will miss it (vv. 27–28).

the sun will be darkened (v. 29)—Such phenomena are a common feature of Day of the Lord prophecy.

from one end of heaven to the other (v. 31)—All the "elect" from heaven and earth are gathered and assembled before Christ; this is the culmination of world history, ushering in the millennial reign of Christ (see Rev. 20:4).

this generation (v. 34)—cannot refer to the generation living at that time of Christ, for "all these things" (vv. 15–31) did not "take place" in their lifetimes; rather a reference to the generation alive at the time when those final hard labor pains begin

day and hour (v. 36)—The precise time was not for them to know; Christ's emphasis instead is on faithfulness, watchfulness, stewardship, expectancy, and preparedness.

26 *"Therefore if they say to you, 'Look, He is in the desert!' do not go out; or 'Look, He is in the inner rooms!' do not believe it.*

27 *For as the lightning comes from the east and flashes to the west, so also will the coming of the Son of Man be.*

28 *For wherever the carcass is, there the eagles will be gathered together.*

29 *"Immediately after the tribulation of those days the sun will be darkened, and the moon will not give its light; the stars will fall from heaven, and the powers of the heavens will be shaken.*

30 *Then the sign of the Son of Man will appear in heaven, and then all the tribes of the earth will mourn, and they will see the Son of Man coming on the clouds of heaven with power and great glory.*

31 *And He will send His angels with a great sound of a trumpet, and they will gather together His elect from the four winds, from one end of heaven to the other.*

32 *"Now learn this parable from the fig tree: When its branch has already become tender and puts forth leaves, you know that summer is near.*

33 *So you also, when you see all these things, know that it is near—at the doors!*

34 *Assuredly, I say to you, this generation will by no means pass away till all these things take place.*

35 *Heaven and earth will pass away, but My words will by no means pass away.*

36 *"But of that day and hour no one knows, not even the angels of heaven, but My Father only.*

37 *But as the days of Noah were, so also will the coming of the Son of Man be.*

38 *For as in the days before the flood, they were eating and drinking, marrying and giving in marriage, until the day that Noah entered the ark,*

39 *and did not know until the flood came and took them all away, so also will the coming of the Son of Man be.*

40 *Then two men will be in the field: one will be taken and the other left.*

41 *Two women will be grinding at the mill: one will be taken and the other left.*

42 *Watch therefore, for you do not know what hour your Lord is coming.*

43 *But know this, that if the master of the house had known what hour the thief would come, he would have watched and not allowed his house to be broken into.*

44 *Therefore you also be ready, for the Son of Man is coming at an hour you do not expect.*

45 *"Who then is a faithful and wise servant, whom his master made ruler over his household, to give them food in due season?*

46 *Blessed is that servant whom his master, when he comes, will find so doing.*

47 *Assuredly, I say to you that he will make him ruler over all his goods.*

48 *But if that evil servant says in his heart, 'My master is delaying his coming,'*

49 *and begins to beat his fellow servants, and to eat and drink with the drunkards,*

50 *the master of that servant will come on a day when he is not looking for him and at an hour that he is not aware of,*

51 *and will cut him in two and appoint him his portion with the hypocrites. There shall be weeping and gnashing of teeth.*

25:1 *"Then the kingdom of heaven shall be likened to ten virgins who took their lamps and went out to meet the bridegroom.*

2 *Now five of them were wise, and five were foolish.*

3 *Those who were foolish took their lamps and took no oil with them,*

4 *but the wise took oil in their vessels with their lamps.*

5 *But while the bridegroom was delayed, they all slumbered and slept.*

one will be taken (vv. 40–41)—taken in judgment (see v. 39); not a reference to the catching away of believers described in 1 Thessalonians 4:16–17

ten virgins (25:1)—i.e., bridesmaids. A Jewish wedding would begin at the bride's house when the bridegroom arrived to observe the wedding ritual. Then a procession would follow as the bridegroom took the bride to his house for the completion of festivities. For a night wedding, "lamps," which were actually torches, were needed for the procession.

6 *"And at midnight a cry was heard: 'Behold, the bridegroom is coming; go out to meet him!'*

7 *Then all those virgins arose and trimmed their lamps.*

8 *And the foolish said to the wise, 'Give us some of your oil, for our lamps are going out.'*

9 *But the wise answered, saying, 'No, lest there should not be enough for us and you; but go rather to those who sell, and buy for yourselves.'*

10 *And while they went to buy, the bridegroom came, and those who were ready went in with him to the wedding; and the door was shut.*

11 *"Afterward the other virgins came also, saying, 'Lord, Lord, open to us!'*

12 *But he answered and said, 'Assuredly, I say to you, I do not know you.'*

13 *"Watch therefore, for you know neither the day nor the hour in which the Son of Man is coming.*

14 *"For the kingdom of heaven is like a man traveling to a far country, who called his own servants and delivered his goods to them.*

talents (v. 15)—A talent was not a gift or ability but a measure of weight, and not a specific coin, so that a talent of gold was more valuable than a talent of silver.

15 *And to one he gave five talents, to another two, and to another one, to each according to his own ability; and immediately he went on a journey.*

16 *Then he who had received the five talents went and traded with them, and made another five talents.*

17 *And likewise he who had received two gained two more also.*

18 *But he who had received one went and dug in the ground, and hid his lord's money.*

19 *After a long time the lord of those servants came and settled accounts with them.*

20 *"So he who had received five talents came and brought five other talents, saying, 'Lord, you delivered to me five talents; look, I have gained five more talents besides them.'*

21 *His lord said to him, 'Well done, good and faithful servant; you were faithful over a few things, I will make you ruler over many things. Enter into the joy of your lord.'*

22 *He also who had received two talents came and said, 'Lord, you delivered to me two talents; look, I have gained two more talents besides them.'*

23 *His lord said to him, 'Well done, good and faithful servant; you have been faithful over a few things, I will make you ruler over many things. Enter into the joy of your lord.'*

24 *"Then he who had received the one talent came and said, 'Lord, I knew you to be a hard man, reaping where you have not sown, and gathering where you have not scattered seed.*

25 *And I was afraid, and went and hid your talent in the ground. Look, there you have what is yours.'*

26 *"But his lord answered and said to him, 'You wicked and lazy servant, you knew that I reap where I have not sown, and gather where I have not scattered seed.*

27 *So you ought to have deposited my money with the bankers, and at my coming I would have received back my own with interest.*

28 *So take the talent from him, and give it to him who has ten talents.*

29 *'For to everyone who has, more will be given, and he will have abundance; but from him who does not have, even what he has will be taken away.*

30 *And cast the unprofitable servant into the outer darkness. There will be weeping and gnashing of teeth.'*

31 *"When the Son of Man comes in His glory, and all the holy angels with Him, then He will sit on the throne of His glory.*

32 *All the nations will be gathered before Him, and He will separate them one from another, as a shepherd divides his sheep from the goats.*

33 *And He will set the sheep on His right hand, but the goats on the left.*

34 *Then the King will say to those on His right hand, 'Come, you blessed of My Father, inherit the kingdom prepared for you from the foundation of the world:*

a hard man (v. 24)—His characterization of the master maligns the man as a cruel and ruthless opportunist, "reaping and gathering" what he had no right to claim as his own; obviously the man has no true knowledge of the master.

to everyone who has, more will be given (v. 29)—Recipients of divine grace inherit immeasurable blessings in addition to eternal life and the favor of God. But those who despise the riches of God's goodness, forbearance, and longsuffering, burying them in the ground and clinging instead to the paltry and transient goods of this world, will ultimately lose everything they have.

He will sit on the throne of His glory (v. 31)—This speaks of the earthly reign of Christ described in Revelation 20:4–6.

Sheep . . . goats (vv. 32–33)—believers and unbelievers, respectively

35 *for I was hungry and you gave Me food; I was thirsty and you gave Me drink; I was a stranger and you took Me in;*

36 *I was naked and you clothed Me; I was sick and you visited Me; I was in prison and you came to Me.'*

37 *"Then the righteous will answer Him, saying, 'Lord, when did we see You hungry and feed You, or thirsty and give You drink?*

38 *When did we see You a stranger and take You in, or naked and clothe You?*

39 *Or when did we see You sick, or in prison, and come to You?'*

40 *And the King will answer and say to them, 'Assuredly, I say to you, inasmuch as you did it to one of the least of these My brethren, you did it to Me.'*

41 *"Then He will also say to those on the left hand, 'Depart from Me, you cursed, into the everlasting fire prepared for the devil and his angels:*

42 *for I was hungry and you gave Me no food; I was thirsty and you gave Me no drink;*

43 *I was a stranger and you did not take Me in, naked and you did not clothe Me, sick and in prison and you did not visit Me.'*

44 *"Then they also will answer Him, saying, 'Lord, when did we see You hungry or thirsty or a stranger or naked or sick or in prison, and did not minister to You?'*

45 *Then He will answer them, saying, 'Assuredly, I say to you, inasmuch as you did not do it to one of the least of these, you did not do it to Me.'*

46 *And these will go away into everlasting punishment, but the righteous into eternal life."*

everlasting punishment . . . eternal life (v. 46)—The same Greek word is used in both instances, suggesting the punishment of the wicked is as never-ending as the bliss of the righteous.

1) How did Jesus describe the Great Tribulation period (24:4–22)?

_____

_____

_____

2) What did Jesus say about His second coming (24:23–31)?

_____

_____

_____

3) According to Jesus, what will be the attitude of most people during the last days?

_____

_____

_____

4) What is the primary lesson in the parable of the ten virgins?

_____

_____

_____

GOING DEEPER

The book of Revelation records a detailed and fascinating account of John's vision of the end times. Read Revelation 6:1–7:12 for a glance at some of the horrors and wonders described.

1 *Now I saw when the Lamb opened one of the seals; and I heard one of the four living creatures saying with a voice like thunder, "Come and see."*
2 *And I looked, and behold, a white horse. He who sat on it had a bow; and a crown was given to him, and he went out conquering and to conquer.*
3 *When He opened the second seal, I heard the second living creature saying, "Come and see."*
4 *Another horse, fiery red, went out. And it was granted to the one who sat on it to take peace from the earth, and that people should kill one another; and there was given to him a great sword.*
5 *When He opened the third seal, I heard the third living creature say, "Come and see." So I looked, and behold, a black horse, and he who sat on it had a pair of scales in his hand.*
6 *And I heard a voice in the midst of the four living creatures saying, "A quart of wheat for a denarius, and three quarts of barley for a denarius; and do not harm the oil and the wine."*

7 When He opened the fourth seal, I heard the voice of the fourth living creature saying, "Come and see."

8 So I looked, and behold, a pale horse. And the name of him who sat on it was Death, and Hades followed with him. And power was given to them over a fourth of the earth, to kill with sword, with hunger, with death, and by the beasts of the earth.

9 When He opened the fifth seal, I saw under the altar the souls of those who had been slain for the word of God and for the testimony which they held.

10 And they cried with a loud voice, saying, "How long, O Lord, holy and true, until You judge and avenge our blood on those who dwell on the earth?"

11 Then a white robe was given to each of them; and it was said to them that they should rest a little while longer, until both the number of their fellow servants and their brethren, who would be killed as they were, was completed.

12 I looked when He opened the sixth seal, and behold, there was a great earthquake; and the sun became black as sackcloth of hair, and the moon became like blood.

13 And the stars of heaven fell to the earth, as a fig tree drops its late figs when it is shaken by a mighty wind.

14 Then the sky receded as a scroll when it is rolled up, and every mountain and island was moved out of its place.

15 And the kings of the earth, the great men, the rich men, the commanders, the mighty men, every slave and every free man, hid themselves in the caves and in the rocks of the mountains,

16 and said to the mountains and rocks, "Fall on us and hide us from the face of Him who sits on the throne and from the wrath of the Lamb!

17 For the great day of His wrath has come, and who is able to stand?"

7:1 After these things I saw four angels standing at the four corners of the earth, holding the four winds of the earth, that the wind should not blow on the earth, on the sea, or on any tree.

2 Then I saw another angel ascending from the east, having the seal of the living God. And he cried with a loud voice to the four angels to whom it was granted to harm the earth and the sea,

3 saying, "Do not harm the earth, the sea, or the trees till we have sealed the servants of our God on their foreheads."

4 And I heard the number of those who were sealed. One hundred and forty-four thousand of all the tribes of the children of Israel were sealed:

5 *of the tribe of Judah twelve thousand were sealed; of the tribe of Reuben twelve thousand were sealed; of the tribe of Gad twelve thousand were sealed;*

6 *of the tribe of Asher twelve thousand were sealed; of the tribe of Naphtali twelve thousand were sealed; of the tribe of Manasseh twelve thousand were sealed;*

7 *of the tribe of Simeon twelve thousand were sealed; of the tribe of Levi twelve thousand were sealed; of the tribe of Issachar twelve thousand were sealed;*

8 *of the tribe of Zebulun twelve thousand were sealed; of the tribe of Joseph twelve thousand were sealed; of the tribe of Benjamin twelve thousand were sealed.*

9 *After these things I looked, and behold, a great multitude which no one could number, of all nations, tribes, peoples, and tongues, standing before the throne and before the Lamb, clothed with white robes, with palm branches in their hands,*

10 *and crying out with a loud voice, saying, "Salvation belongs to our God who sits on the throne, and to the Lamb!"*

11 *All the angels stood around the throne and the elders and the four living creatures, and fell on their faces before the throne and worshiped God,*

12 *saying: "Amen! Blessing and glory and wisdom, thanksgiving and honor and power and might, be to our God forever and ever. Amen."*

EXPLORING THE MEANING

5) How does this description in Revelation compare with Jesus' description of the last days in Matthew 24:5–30?

_____

_____

_____

_____

6) The parable of the fig tree is extremely brief (24:32–35). What message is Jesus conveying in these few words?

_____

_____

_____

7) What "generation" is Jesus referring to in Matthew 24:34?

_____

_____

_____

_____

_____

8) How can we know the taking away of people in Matthew 24:39–41 is a taking away of unbelievers into judgment and not a snatching away of believers in the Rapture (see 1 Thess. 4:16–17)?

_____

_____

_____

_____

9) How would you explain the parable of the talents to a new Christian?

_____

_____

_____

_____

_____

TRUTH FOR TODAY

The theme of Christ's second coming permeates the New Testament and is the great anticipatory reality of Christian living. The Lord's return will be as real and as historical an event as His first coming. Believers look *back* to the moment of saving faith in Christ, when their souls were redeemed. They look *forward* to the return of Christ, when their bodies will be redeemed and they will enter into the promised fullness of salvation. In that day Satan will be defeated, the curse lifted, Christ worshiped, the creation liberated and restored, sin and death conquered, and the saints glorified.

REFLECTING ON THE TEXT

10) In what specific ways can studying and reflecting on Bible prophecy motivate us to live differently?

_____

_____

_____

_____

_____

_____

11) How can a Christian know when he or she is being watchful as prescribed in these chapters?

_____

_____

_____

_____

_____

12) What specific changes do you need to make in your life in light of this study of Matthew 24–25?

_____

_____

_____

_____

_____

_____

PERSONAL RESPONSE

Write out additional reflections, questions you may have, or a prayer.

_____

_____

_____

_____

_____

_____

_____

_____

_____

_____

_____

_____

_____

_____

_____

_____

_____

_____

_____

_____

_____

_____

_____

SUFFERING SAVIOR ... RISEN LORD

Matthew 26:1–28:20

DRAWING NEAR

When have you been most moved by Christ's sacrifice for you (e.g., during a sermon, a movie about the life of Christ, taking communion, or other)? What about that experience made it more meaningful?

_____

_____

_____

THE CONTEXT

Matthew 26 begins the final and most pivotal section of this Gospel. Everything else has been a prologue, an introduction to the great conclusion, which focuses on the cross of Jesus Christ—the culmination of this book, the culmination of redemptive history, and the only eternal hope of fallen mankind. Everything in the sacred story of God's redemptive plan does indeed center on the cross. It is through the cross of Christ alone that the Lord has provided the way for sinners to be saved and united with Him, the holy God. There is no salvation, no gospel, no biblical Christianity apart from the cross of Christ.

Matthew deals with the cross in a concise and straightforward way. He details the preparation for the cross and the arrest of Jesus. He presents Jesus' trials, execution, and burial. Then he narrates the Lord's resurrection victory over death and His final triumphant instructions to the disciples.

KEYS TO THE TEXT

Jesus' Death: There were many times when people sought to kill Jesus but were unable to do so. The Jewish religious leaders began plotting His death soon after He began His public ministry (John 5:18), but they were not able to fulfill that intention until it fit into God's timetable. The first attempt on Jesus' life was made shortly after He was born, when Herod massacred all the male infants in the vicinity of Bethlehem. God sent an angel to warn Joseph to take Jesus and His mother to Egypt until the danger was over. On one occasion the people became incensed by His claim to be fulfilling Isaiah's prophecy. They succeeded in leading Him to the edge of a high cliff on the outskirts of the city, but before

139

they could throw Him to His death, He miraculously passed through their midst and went His way (Luke 4:16–30). After Jesus healed the crippled man at the pool of Bethesda, the Jewish leaders began seeking "all the more to kill Him, because He not only broke the Sabbath, but also said that God was His Father, making Himself equal with God" (John 5:18 NKJV).

All of those attempts to kill Jesus failed because it was not God's time or God's way for the Son to die. Only the sovereign grace of God could have brought Jesus to the cross. No human power could have accomplished it apart from God's will, and no human power could now prevent it, because it was now God's plan. The appropriate time for Jesus to die was at Passover, when the sacrificial lambs were slain, because that celebration pointed to "the Lamb of God who takes away the sin of the world!" (John 1:29 NKJV). The sacrifices of all the other lambs were but faint symbols of what the true Lamb was soon to accomplish in reality.

UNLEASHING THE TEXT

Read 26:1–28:20, noting the key words and definitions next to the passage.

Matthew 26:1–28:20 (NKJV)

Passover (26:2)—This was God's chosen time for Christ to die; He was the antitype to which the Passover Lamb had always referred (John 1:29).

1 Now it came to pass, when Jesus had finished all these sayings, that He said to His disciples,

2 "You know that after two days is the Passover, and the Son of Man will be delivered up to be crucified."

3 Then the chief priests, the scribes, and the elders of the people assembled at the palace of the high priest, who was called Caiaphas,

4 and plotted to take Jesus by trickery and kill Him.

5 But they said, "Not during the feast, lest there be an uproar among the people."

6 And when Jesus was in Bethany at the house of Simon the leper,

7 a woman came to Him having an alabaster flask of very costly fragrant oil, and she poured it on His head as He sat at the table.

8 But when His disciples saw it, they were indignant, saying, "Why this waste?

9 For this fragrant oil might have been sold for much and given to the poor."

10 But when Jesus was aware of it, He said to them, "Why do you trouble the woman? For she has done a good work for Me.

11 *For you have the poor with you always, but Me you do not have always.*

12 *For in pouring this fragrant oil on My body, she did it for My burial.*

13 *Assuredly, I say to you, wherever this gospel is preached in the whole world, what this woman has done will also be told as a memorial to her."*

14 *Then one of the twelve, called Judas Iscariot, went to the chief priests*

15 *and said, "What are you willing to give me if I deliver Him to you?" And they counted out to him thirty pieces of silver.*

16 *So from that time he sought opportunity to betray Him.*

17 *Now on the first day of the Feast of Unleavened Bread the disciples came to Jesus, saying to Him, "Where do You want us to prepare for You to eat the Passover?"*

18 *And He said, "Go into the city to a certain man, and say to him, 'The Teacher says, "My time is at hand; I will keep the Passover at your house with My disciples."'"*

19 *So the disciples did as Jesus had directed them; and they prepared the Passover.*

20 *When evening had come, He sat down with the twelve.*

21 *Now as they were eating, He said, "Assuredly, I say to you, one of you will betray Me."*

22 *And they were exceedingly sorrowful, and each of them began to say to Him, "Lord, is it I?"*

23 *He answered and said, "He who dipped his hand with Me in the dish will betray Me.*

24 *The Son of Man indeed goes just as it is written of Him, but woe to that man by whom the Son of Man is betrayed! It would have been good for that man if he had not been born."*

25 *Then Judas, who was betraying Him, answered and said, "Rabbi, is it I?" He said to him, "You have said it."*

26 *And as they were eating, Jesus took bread, blessed and broke it, and gave it to the disciples and said, "Take, eat; this is My body."*

For you have the poor with you always (v. 11)—Jesus certainly was not disparaging ministry to the poor; however, He revealed here that there is a higher priority than any other earthly ministry, and that is worship rendered to Him.

a memorial to her (v. 13)—This promise was guaranteed by the inclusion of this story in the New Testament.

Take, eat; this is My body (v. 26)—Jesus thus transformed the last Passover into the first observance of the Lord's Supper.

My blood of the new covenant (v. 28)—The blood of the new covenant is not an animal's blood, but Christ's own blood, shed for the remission of sins.

sung a hymn (v. 30)—probably Psalm 118

Gethsemane (v. 36)—literally, "oil press," a frequent meeting place for Christ and His disciples, just across the Kidron Valley from Jerusalem

not as I will, but as You will (v. 39)—This implies no conflict between the Persons of the Godhead. Rather, it graphically reveals how Christ in His humanity voluntarily surrendered His will to the will of the Father in all things.

27 Then He took the cup, and gave thanks, and gave it to them, saying, "Drink from it, all of you.

28 For this is My blood of the new covenant, which is shed for many for the remission of sins.

29 But I say to you, I will not drink of this fruit of the vine from now on until that day when I drink it new with you in My Father's kingdom."

30 And when they had sung a hymn, they went out to the Mount of Olives.

31 Then Jesus said to them, "All of you will be made to stumble because of Me this night, for it is written: 'I will strike the Shepherd, And the sheep of the flock will be scattered.'

32 But after I have been raised, I will go before you to Galilee."

33 Peter answered and said to Him, "Even if all are made to stumble because of You, I will never be made to stumble."

34 Jesus said to him, "Assuredly, I say to you that this night, before the rooster crows, you will deny Me three times."

35 Peter said to Him, "Even if I have to die with You, I will not deny You!" And so said all the disciples.

36 Then Jesus came with them to a place called Gethsemane, and said to the disciples, "Sit here while I go and pray over there."

37 And He took with Him Peter and the two sons of Zebedee, and He began to be sorrowful and deeply distressed.

38 Then He said to them, "My soul is exceedingly sorrowful, even to death. Stay here and watch with Me."

39 He went a little farther and fell on His face, and prayed, saying, "O My Father, if it is possible, let this cup pass from Me; nevertheless, not as I will, but as You will."

40 Then He came to the disciples and found them sleeping, and said to Peter, "What! Could you not watch with Me one hour?

41 *Watch and pray, lest you enter into temptation. The spirit indeed is willing, but the flesh is weak."*

42 *Again, a second time, He went away and prayed, saying, "O My Father, if this cup cannot pass away from Me unless I drink it, Your will be done."*

43 *And He came and found them asleep again, for their eyes were heavy.*

44 *So He left them, went away again, and prayed the third time, saying the same words.*

45 *Then He came to His disciples and said to them, "Are you still sleeping and resting? Behold, the hour is at hand, and the Son of Man is being betrayed into the hands of sinners.*

46 *Rise, let us be going. See, My betrayer is at hand."*

47 *And while He was still speaking, behold, Judas, one of the twelve, with a great multitude with swords and clubs, came from the chief priests and elders of the people.*

Judas, one of the twelve (v. 47)— The expression underscores the insidiousness of Judas's crime— especially here, in the midst of the betrayal.

48 *Now His betrayer had given them a sign, saying, "Whomever I kiss, He is the One; seize Him."*

49 *Immediately he went up to Jesus and said, "Greetings, Rabbi!" and kissed Him.*

50 *But Jesus said to him, "Friend, why have you come?" Then they came and laid hands on Jesus and took Him.*

51 *And suddenly, one of those who were with Jesus stretched out his hand and drew his sword, struck the servant of the high priest, and cut off his ear.*

52 *But Jesus said to him, "Put your sword in its place, for all who take the sword will perish by the sword.*

53 *Or do you think that I cannot now pray to My Father, and He will provide Me with more than twelve legions of angels?*

more than twelve legions (v. 53)—A Roman legion was composed of 6,000 soldiers, so this would represent more than 72,000 angels.

54 *How then could the Scriptures be fulfilled, that it must happen thus?"*

55 *In that hour Jesus said to the multitudes, "Have you come out, as against a robber, with swords and clubs to take Me? I sat daily with you, teaching in the temple, and you did not seize Me.*

Scriptures be fulfilled (v. 54)— God Himself had foreordained the very minutest details of how Jesus would die, and everyone around Him—His enemies included—fulfilled precisely the details of the Old Testament prophecies.

the council (v. 59)—The Sanhedrin was the Supreme Court of Israel, consisting of seventy-one members, presided over by the high priest.

they found none (v. 60)—Even though many were willing to perjure themselves, the Sanhedrin could not find a charge that had enough credibility to indict Jesus; the "false witnesses" could not agree among themselves.

56 But all this was done that the Scriptures of the prophets might be fulfilled." Then all the disciples forsook Him and fled.

57 And those who had laid hold of Jesus led Him away to Caiaphas the high priest, where the scribes and the elders were assembled.

58 But Peter followed Him at a distance to the high priest's courtyard. And he went in and sat with the servants to see the end.

59 Now the chief priests, the elders, and all the council sought false testimony against Jesus to put Him to death,

60 but found none. Even though many false witnesses came forward, they found none. But at last two false witnesses came forward

61 and said, "This fellow said, 'I am able to destroy the temple of God and to build it in three days.' "

62 And the high priest arose and said to Him, "Do You answer nothing? What is it these men testify against You?"

63 But Jesus kept silent. And the high priest answered and said to Him, "I put You under oath by the living God: Tell us if You are the Christ, the Son of God!"

64 Jesus said to him, "It is as you said. Nevertheless, I say to you, hereafter you will see the Son of Man sitting at the right hand of the Power, and coming on the clouds of heaven."

65 Then the high priest tore his clothes, saying, "He has spoken blasphemy! What further need do we have of witnesses? Look, now you have heard His blasphemy!

66 What do you think?" They answered and said, "He is deserving of death."

67 Then they spat in His face and beat Him; and others struck Him with the palms of their hands,

68 saying, "Prophesy to us, Christ! Who is the one who struck You?"

69 Now Peter sat outside in the courtyard. And a servant girl came to him, saying, "You also were with Jesus of Galilee."

70 *But he denied it before them all, saying, "I do not know what you are saying."*

71 *And when he had gone out to the gateway, another girl saw him and said to those who were there, "This fellow also was with Jesus of Nazareth."*

72 *But again he denied with an oath, "I do not know the Man!"*

73 *And a little later those who stood by came up and said to Peter, "Surely you also are one of them, for your speech betrays you."*

74 *Then he began to curse and swear, saying, "I do not know the Man!" Immediately a rooster crowed.*

75 *And Peter remembered the word of Jesus who had said to him, "Before the rooster crows, you will deny Me three times." So he went out and wept bitterly.*

27:1 *When morning came, all the chief priests and elders of the people plotted against Jesus to put Him to death.*

2 *And when they had bound Him, they led Him away and delivered Him to Pontius Pilate the governor.*

3 *Then Judas, His betrayer, seeing that He had been condemned, was remorseful and brought back the thirty pieces of silver to the chief priests and elders,*

4 *saying, "I have sinned by betraying innocent blood." And they said, "What is that to us? You see to it!"*

5 *Then he threw down the pieces of silver in the temple and departed, and went and hanged himself.*

6 *But the chief priests took the silver pieces and said, "It is not lawful to put them into the treasury, because they are the price of blood."*

7 *And they consulted together and bought with them the potter's field, to bury strangers in.*

8 *Therefore that field has been called the Field of Blood to this day.*

9 *Then was fulfilled what was spoken by Jeremiah the prophet, saying, "And they took the thirty pieces of silver, the value of Him who was priced, whom they of the children of Israel priced,*

10 *and gave them for the potter's field, as the LORD directed me."*

he began to curse and swear (v. 74)—Calling on God as His witness, he declared, "I do not know the Man!" and pronounced a curse of death on himself at God's hand if his words were untrue.

And Peter remembered (v. 75)—Luke 22:61 records that Jesus made eye contact with Peter at this very moment, which must have magnified Peter's already unbearable sense of shame.

remorseful (v. 3)—Judas felt the sting of his own guilt, but this was not genuine repentance.

11 *Now Jesus stood before the governor. And the governor asked Him, saying, "Are You the King of the Jews?" Jesus said to him, "It is as you say."*

12 *And while He was being accused by the chief priests and elders, He answered nothing.*

13 *Then Pilate said to Him, "Do You not hear how many things they testify against You?"*

14 *But He answered him not one word, so that the governor marveled greatly.*

15 *Now at the feast the governor was accustomed to releasing to the multitude one prisoner whom they wished.*

16 *And at that time they had a notorious prisoner called Barabbas.*

17 *Therefore, when they had gathered together, Pilate said to them, "Whom do you want me to release to you? Barabbas, or Jesus who is called Christ?"*

18 *For he knew that they had handed Him over because of envy.*

19 *While he was sitting on the judgment seat, his wife sent to him, saying, "Have nothing to do with that just Man, for I have suffered many things today in a dream because of Him."*

20 *But the chief priests and elders persuaded the multitudes that they should ask for Barabbas and destroy Jesus.*

21 *The governor answered and said to them, "Which of the two do you want me to release to you?" They said, "Barabbas!"*

22 *Pilate said to them, "What then shall I do with Jesus who is called Christ?" They all said to him, "Let Him be crucified!"*

23 *Then the governor said, "Why, what evil has He done?" But they cried out all the more, saying, "Let Him be crucified!"*

24 *When Pilate saw that he could not prevail at all, but rather that a tumult was rising, he took water and washed his hands before the multitude, saying, "I am innocent of the blood of this just Person. You see to it."*

25 *And all the people answered and said, "His blood be on us and on our children."*

26 *Then he released Barabbas to them; and when he had scourged Jesus, he delivered Him to be crucified.*

27 *Then the soldiers of the governor took Jesus into the Praetorium and gathered the whole garrison around Him.*

28 *And they stripped Him and put a scarlet robe on Him.*

29 *When they had twisted a crown of thorns, they put it on His head, and a reed in His right hand. And they bowed the knee before Him and mocked Him, saying, "Hail, King of the Jews!"*

30 *Then they spat on Him, and took the reed and struck Him on the head.*

31 *And when they had mocked Him, they took the robe off Him, put His own clothes on Him, and led Him away to be crucified.*

32 *Now as they came out, they found a man of Cyrene, Simon by name. Him they compelled to bear His cross.*

33 *And when they had come to a place called Golgotha, that is to say, Place of a Skull,*

34 *they gave Him sour wine mingled with gall to drink. But when He had tasted it, He would not drink.*

35 *Then they crucified Him, and divided His garments, casting lots, that it might be fulfilled which was spoken by the prophet: "They divided My garments among them, And for My clothing they cast lots."*

36 *Sitting down, they kept watch over Him there.*

37 *And they put up over His head the accusation written against Him: THIS IS JESUS THE KING OF THE JEWS.*

38 *Then two robbers were crucified with Him, one on the right and another on the left.*

39 *And those who passed by blasphemed Him, wagging their heads*

40 *and saying, "You who destroy the temple and build it in three days, save Yourself! If You are the Son of God, come down from the cross."*

scourged (v. 26)—The whip used consisted of several strands of leather, each with a bit of metal or bone attached to the end. The process would tear the flesh from the back, lacerating muscles, and sometimes even exposing the kidneys or other internal organs; it was often fatal.

Praetorium (v. 27)—Pilate's residence in Jerusalem

a reed in His right hand (v. 30)—To imitate a scepter, they purposely chose something flimsy looking.

to be crucified (v. 31)—Roman executioners had perfected the art of slow torture while keeping crucifixion victims alive; most hung on the cross for days before dying of exhaustion, dehydration, traumatic fever, or—most likely—suffocation.

Place of a Skull (v. 33)—"Golgotha" may have been a skull-shaped hill, or it may have been so named because as a place of crucifixion, it accumulated skulls.

divided His garments (v. 35)—The garments of the victim were the customary spoils of the executioners; foretold in Psalm 22:18.

Likewise the chief priests also, mocking with the scribes and elders, said,

42 "He saved others; Himself He cannot save. If He is the King of Israel, let Him now come down from the cross, and we will believe Him.

43 He trusted in God; let Him deliver Him now if He will have Him; for He said, 'I am the Son of God.' "

44 Even the robbers who were crucified with Him reviled Him with the same thing.

45 Now from the sixth hour until the ninth hour there was darkness over all the land.

46 And about the ninth hour Jesus cried out with a loud voice, saying, "Eli, Eli, lama sabachthani?" that is, "My God, My God, why have You forsaken Me?"

47 Some of those who stood there, when they heard that, said, "This Man is calling for Elijah!"

48 Immediately one of them ran and took a sponge, filled it with sour wine and put it on a reed, and offered it to Him to drink.

49 The rest said, "Let Him alone; let us see if Elijah will come to save Him."

50 And Jesus cried out again with a loud voice, and yielded up His spirit.

51 Then, behold, the veil of the temple was torn in two from top to bottom; and the earth quaked, and the rocks were split,

52 and the graves were opened; and many bodies of the saints who had fallen asleep were raised;

53 and coming out of the graves after His resurrection, they went into the holy city and appeared to many.

54 So when the centurion and those with him, who were guarding Jesus, saw the earthquake and the things that had happened, they feared greatly, saying, "Truly this was the Son of God!"

55 And many women who followed Jesus from Galilee, ministering to Him, were there looking on from afar,

56 among whom were Mary Magdalene, Mary the mother of James and Joses, and the mother of Zebedee's sons.

Eli, Eli, lama sabachthani (v. 46)—This is a fulfillment of Psalm 22:1. Christ at that moment was experiencing the abandonment and despair that resulted from the outpouring of divine wrath on Him as sin-bearer.

the veil of the temple (v. 51)—The tearing of the curtain that blocked the entrance to the Most Holy Place signified that the way into God's presence was now open to all through a new and living way (Heb. 10:19–22); the fact that it tore "from top to bottom" showed that God did it.

bodies of the saints . . . were raised (v. 52)—Matthew alone mentions this miracle. Nothing more is said about these people, which would be unlikely if they remained on earth for long. Evidently, these people were given glorified bodies; they appeared "to many" (v. 53), enough to establish the reality of the miracle; and then they no doubt ascended to glory—a kind of foretaste of 1 Thessalonians 4:16.

57 *Now when evening had come, there came a rich man from Arimathea, named Joseph, who himself had also become a disciple of Jesus.*

58 *This man went to Pilate and asked for the body of Jesus. Then Pilate commanded the body to be given to him.*

59 *When Joseph had taken the body, he wrapped it in a clean linen cloth,*

60 *and laid it in his new tomb which he had hewn out of the rock; and he rolled a large stone against the door of the tomb, and departed.*

61 *And Mary Magdalene was there, and the other Mary, sitting opposite the tomb.*

62 *On the next day, which followed the Day of Preparation, the chief priests and Pharisees gathered together to Pilate,*

63 *saying, "Sir, we remember, while He was still alive, how that deceiver said, 'After three days I will rise.'*

64 *Therefore command that the tomb be made secure until the third day, lest His disciples come by night and steal Him away, and say to the people, 'He has risen from the dead.' So the last deception will be worse than the first."*

65 *Pilate said to them, "You have a guard; go your way, make it as secure as you know how."*

66 *So they went and made the tomb secure, sealing the stone and setting the guard.*

28:1 *Now after the Sabbath, as the first day of the week began to dawn, Mary Magdalene and the other Mary came to see the tomb.*

2 *And behold, there was a great earthquake; for an angel of the Lord descended from heaven, and came and rolled back the stone from the door, and sat on it.*

3 *His countenance was like lightning, and his clothing as white as snow.*

4 *And the guards shook for fear of him, and became like dead men.*

5 *But the angel answered and said to the women, "Do not be afraid, for I know that you seek Jesus who was crucified.*

Joseph (v. 57)—a member of the Sanhedrin who had not consented to their condemning Christ

as the first day of the week began to dawn (28:1)—Sabbath officially ended with sundown on Saturday; at that time the women could purchase and prepare spices.

became like dead men (v. 4)—not merely paralyzed with fear, but completely unconscious, totally traumatized by what they had seen

reported to the chief priests (v. 11)—The Jewish leaders' determination to cover up what had occurred reveals the obstinacy of unbelief in the face of overwhelming evidence.

while we slept (v. 13)—This was not a very good cover-up; how could they know what had happened while they were asleep?

the eleven disciples (v. 16)—The fact that some there "doubted" (v. 17) strongly suggests that more than the Eleven were present; possibly several hundred (see 1 Cor. 15:6).

All authority (v. 20)—Absolute sovereign authority—lordship over all—is handed to Christ.

I am with you (v. 20)—Here is a touching echo of the beginning of Matthew's gospel. *Immanuel* (1:23) "which is translated 'God with us'"—remains "with" us "even to the end of the age."

6 *He is not here; for He is risen, as He said. Come, see the place where the Lord lay.*

7 *And go quickly and tell His disciples that He is risen from the dead, and indeed He is going before you into Galilee; there you will see Him. Behold, I have told you."*

8 *So they went out quickly from the tomb with fear and great joy, and ran to bring His disciples word.*

9 *And as they went to tell His disciples, behold, Jesus met them, saying, "Rejoice!" So they came and held Him by the feet and worshiped Him.*

10 *Then Jesus said to them, "Do not be afraid. Go and tell My brethren to go to Galilee, and there they will see Me."*

11 *Now while they were going, behold, some of the guard came into the city and reported to the chief priests all the things that had happened.*

12 *When they had assembled with the elders and consulted together, they gave a large sum of money to the soldiers,*

13 *saying, "Tell them, 'His disciples came at night and stole Him away while we slept.'*

14 *And if this comes to the governor's ears, we will appease him and make you secure."*

15 *So they took the money and did as they were instructed; and this saying is commonly reported among the Jews until this day.*

16 *Then the eleven disciples went away into Galilee, to the mountain which Jesus had appointed for them.*

17 *When they saw Him, they worshiped Him; but some doubted.*

18 *And Jesus came and spoke to them, saying, "All authority has been given to Me in heaven and on earth.*

19 *Go therefore and make disciples of all the nations, baptizing them in the name of the Father and of the Son and of the Holy Spirit,*

20 *teaching them to observe all things that I have commanded you; and lo, I am with you always, even to the end of the age." Amen.*

1) What happened when Mary anointed Jesus? What was the reaction?

_____

_____

_____

2) Summarize the experience of Peter in these final three chapters of Matthew? What range of emotions did he go through?

_____

_____

_____

3) How would you characterize Christ's mood or demeanor during these final hours of His life? What emotions does He reveal? How does He demonstrate resolve?

_____

_____

_____

4) What detail(s) about Jesus' arrest, trial, and crucifixion, did you notice for the first time?

_____

_____

_____

GOING DEEPER

Read Isaiah 52:13–53:12 for Isaiah's prophetic words that relate to this passage in Matthew.

13 *Behold, My Servant shall deal prudently; He shall be exalted and extolled and be very high.*

14 *Just as many were astonished at you, so His visage was marred more than any man, and His form more than the sons of men;*

15 *So shall He sprinkle many nations. Kings shall shut their mouths at Him; for what had not been told them they shall see, And what they had not heard they shall consider.*

53:1 *Who has believed our report? And to whom has the arm of the LORD been revealed?*

2 *For He shall grow up before Him as a tender plant, and as a root out of dry ground. He has no form or comeliness; and when we see Him, there is no beauty that we should desire Him.*

3 *He is despised and rejected by men, a Man of sorrows and acquainted with grief. And we hid, as it were, our faces from Him; He was despised, and we did not esteem Him.*

4 *Surely He has borne our griefs and carried our sorrows; yet we esteemed Him stricken, smitten by God, and afflicted.*

5 *But He was wounded for our transgressions, He was bruised for our iniquities; the chastisement for our peace was upon Him, and by His stripes we are healed.*

6 *All we like sheep have gone astray; we have turned, every one, to his own way; and the LORD has laid on Him the iniquity of us all.*

7 *He was oppressed and He was afflicted, yet He opened not His mouth; He was led as a lamb to the slaughter, and as a sheep before its shearers is silent, so He opened not His mouth.*

8 *He was taken from prison and from judgment, and who will declare His generation? For He was cut off from the land of the living; for the transgressions of My people He was stricken.*

9 *And they made His grave with the wicked—but with the rich at His death, because He had done no violence, Nor was any deceit in His mouth.*

10 *Yet it pleased the LORD to bruise Him; He has put Him to grief. When You make His soul an offering for sin, He shall see His seed, He shall prolong His days, and the pleasure of the LORD shall prosper in His hand.*

11 *He shall see the labor of His soul, and be satisfied. By His knowledge My righteous Servant shall justify many, for He shall bear their iniquities.*

12 *Therefore I will divide Him a portion with the great, and He shall divide the spoil with the strong, because He poured out His soul unto death, and He was numbered with the transgressors, and He bore the sin of many, and made intercession for the transgressors.*

EXPLORING THE MEANING

5) Note the many ways that Christ's crucifixion fulfilled the details of this ancient prophecy.

_____

_____

_____

6) Why do you think Peter failed so badly during this critical time? One minute he is wielding a sword to protect Jesus; the next he is swearing that he doesn't even know Jesus. What do you make of this?

_____

_____

_____

7) Review all the supernatural events that took place around the time of the resurrection. What do they signify?

_____

_____

_____

8) Mark 15:43 and Luke 23:50–51 identify Joseph of Arimathea, the "disciple of Jesus," as a member of the Jewish Sanhedrin. Why is this significant?

_____

_____

_____

9) What are the main ideas conveyed in Matthew 28?

_____

_____

_____

TRUTH FOR TODAY

The Great Commission (Matt. 28:19–20) is a command to bring unbelievers throughout the world to a saving knowledge of Jesus Christ. The true convert is a _disciple_, a person who has accepted and submitted himself to Jesus Christ, and all that may mean or demand. The truly converted person is filled with the Holy Spirit and given a new nature that yearns to obey and worship the Lord who has saved him. Even when he is disobedient, he knows he is living against the grain of his new nature, which is to honor and please the Lord. He loves righteousness and hates sin, including his own.

Jesus' supreme command, therefore, is for those who are His disciples to become His instruments for making disciples of all nations. Jesus' own earthly ministry was to make disciples for Himself, and that is the ministry of His people. Those who truly follow Jesus Christ become "fishers of men" (Matt. 4:19). The mission of the early church was to make disciples (see Acts 2:47; 14:21), and that is still Christ's mission for His church.

REFLECTING ON THE TEXT

10) What steps can you take to guard against the kind of fear and weakness displayed by all the disciples?

_____

_____

_____

11) Standing there looking at the resurrected Lord, the text says some of the disciples "worshiped Him; but some doubted" (Matt. 28:17). How do you explain this?

_____

_____

_____

12) What does the Great Commission look like in your life today? How are you involved in making disciples? How can you begin to live out that broad command from our King of kings?

_____

_____

_____

PERSONAL RESPONSE

Write out additional reflections, questions you may have, or a prayer.

_____

_____

_____

_____

Look for these exciting titles by John MacArthur

Experiencing the Passion of Christ

Experiencing the Passion of Christ Student Edition

Twelve Extraordinary Women Workbook

Twelve Ordinary Men Workbook

Welcome to the Family:
What to Expect Now That You're a Christian

What the Bible Says About Parenting:
Biblical Principles for Raising Godly Children

Hard to Believe Workbook:
The High Cost and Infinite Value of Following Jesus

The John MacArthur Study Library for PDA

The MacArthur Bible Commentary

The MacArthur Study Bible, NKJV

The MacArthur Topical Bible, NKJV

The MacArthur Bible Commentary

The MacArthur Bible Handbook

The MacArthur Bible Studies series

Available at your local Christian bookstore
or visit www.thomasnelson.com